Letters from Leiper's Fork

Wayne Christeson

Books Fluent
25 Main St. Suite B1
Nashville TN 37206

Copyright @ 2020 Wayne Christeson
www.lettersfromleipersfork.com

First Edition
Paperback ISBN 978-1-7352689-5-8
E-Book ISBN 978-1-7352689-6-5
Library of Congress Control Number 9781735268958

For my darlin' Anne,
my heart and soul

Also for
Bruce and Marty Hunt,
the heart and soul
of Leiper's Fork

Tis strange—but true;
For truth is always strange;
Stranger than fiction

—*George Gordon*, Lord Byron

Contents

Author's Preface

Where in the hell is Leiper's Fork?

That's what our friends from Nashville used to ask us when we moved here thirty years ago. It's a good question because it doesn't really have a clear answer. In those days, Leiper's Fork was not identified on traditional road maps and if you wandered around looking for it, you probably wouldn't find it. But if you became well and truly lost, you might perhaps stumble into it. As my friend Aubrey Preston used to say, "Leiper's Fork is a state of mind," and he's not far wrong.

In the old days, when we arrived, the town was just a dusty little farming community where artists and musicians hung out. "Downtown" Leiper's Fork was a small cluster of old houses and some aging commercial buildings. There was one genuine grocery store, an antique store, a guitar shop, and a short order restaurant, along with a vacant service station, a tumble-down roofing building, an unused laundromat, and other assorted empty places.

One reason the community was so difficult to find was that it had two names. If outsiders asked the locals, "Where in the hell is Leiper's Fork?" our neighbors might reply, truthfully, "There ain't no such place." At least to them there wasn't. You see, for almost 100 years the community had been known to everyone as "Hillsboro." But one day a man from the post office came to town and said, "There's another town down near Fayetteville called Hillsborough, so we're going to change your name. From henceforth this town shall be known as Leiper's Fork." Period. That was it. Nobody even got to vote on it.

Changing the name of your home community, of course, is a pretty drastic event—kind of like changing your family name or the name of you first child. It has taken a generation for local people to begin adjusting to it. There are a few cantankerous folks from the older families who continue to say "Hillsboro" as a matter of pride and personal identification. But they are outliers.

Along with its name, the town has changed so completely over the past thirty years that the old community is no longer recognizable. The tangled web of families and kinships are gone, as is the life they followed. The stories of these people are the stories of a special time in the history of a small, distant place, before it grew into the tourist destination it is now. And those stories should be recorded and passed down.

That's why I'm writing this book. All these stories are true, as improbable as they may seem. I either participated in them or witnessed them, or heard of them on good authority.

I knew and loved these people. They were my neighbors and my friends.

WAYNE CHRISTESON
LEIPER'S FORK, TENNESSEE
OCTOBER 2020

Chapter 1

Shoot Your Computer

I n the end, Bruce Hunt took to calling the printer Old Rattler, since it shivered to life like Tom Osborn's pick-up every time he fired it up.

Bruce is a legend around Leiper's Fork. He features himself as an irascible old-time, hand-tool craftsman—old school to the core. But most people know that lurking behind his pale blue eyes is a mind sharp enough to gut a fish. So it hasn't surprised me that he has recently been drawn into the spider web of computer technology. He has a powerful applied curiosity, and he clearly relishes the complex problems the computer poses. He tangles with these electronic tar-babies just for the fun of it.

The printer was actually mine to begin with, and let me tell you, Old Rattler was a tar baby of the first order. I laid down $135 for it at Office Depot after the salesman told me it was the high end of the Hewlett-Packard line. And it sure looked good when I brought it home and installed it on my writing table.

It was a tasteful, plum-colored swoop of curved and beveled plastic. It looked as svelte and powerful as an old Packard automobile. It featured multi-colored printing and two-sided printing; it could print envelopes and banners, greeting cards, and probably the Declaration of Independence. And best of all, it was stamped with the Hewlett-Packard name.

The only problem was that it wouldn't work. It wouldn't move or produce anything. Every time I tried to use it, the best that it could do was moan and sigh. I fiddled with several software ideas, but I got nowhere. I rigged and re-rigged the wiring. I even tried slapping it on the side and spitting in the back like Andy Griffith used to do.

But nothing helped. It got to the point that the printer would strain and snap anytime I tried to make it work. And it would shake and rattle so violently that I had to shut it off to keep it from breaking up entirely. The poor thing was trying so hard and its suffering was so obvious, that I actually began to feel sorry for it.

In today's electronic world, of course, nobody knew how to fix it, since nobody outside of China knew how it was made. The warranty covered almost nothing, of course, so I had little choice but to buy a new printer and let the old one go. It was a hard decision to make.

I went to a different computer store this time, and once again, I let the salesman talk me into buying a Hewlett-Packard. This one was more expensive than the first one, but the salesman assured me that it was better. (You've got to understand, of course, that "salesmen" in computer stores are generally lax, pale, acned zombies about half my age whose standard expression is, "Yeah, sure, dude, that'll work . . .")

So I paid up and left with the new printer and the old one under each arm. I didn't give any thought to what I might do with the old one, since, theoretically, it was still a working printer.

Then, as I was driving through Leiper's Fork toward home, I saw Bruce eating his lunch in the sun outside Puckett's, and an idea began to form in my mind. I decided that I would stop and show Bruce the new printer and then casually mention that we ought to take the old printer down to the creek and shoot it. It would be the respectful thing to do. And it would be fun.

As I knew he would, Bruce frowned and said, "Wayne, you can't just throw that thing away. Let's carry it on down to my barn and see if we can make it work." I figured that would be more entertaining than shooting the printer, since watching Bruce revive inert equipment is one of the great pleasures of life.

After lunch we drove down to Bruce's barn and, of course, the minute Bruce plugged it in the printer began to run with a soft satisfying hum. I can't say I was surprised, since I know Bruce has a talent for charming all kinds of worn-out things into motion—that's how he keeps his own ramshackle body moving.

But I warned Bruce that this machine was not above performing a hustle on him. "Just wait a while," I said, "and see what happens." But Bruce was confident, so I told him he could keep the thing, and I left shaking my head. Surely this couldn't last.

I heard a lot from Bruce about that printer over the next few weeks—progress reports, you might say. He'd never miss a chance to tell me what a great little printer I had given him. He was real tickled and had great plans for it.

After a while, though, I began to notice that Bruce spoke less and less about the printer and that there was a twinge of sadness in his voice when he did. He finally admitted that the printer had started seizing up on him. He spoke about it in the concerned and puzzled voice of someone whose well had run dry or whose chickens wouldn't lay.

As I listened to Bruce, it dawned on me that he had developed a genuine fondness for that cranky old printer. Bruce carries a blood affinity for anything that is contrary and difficult, and it seemed as though he had adopted the printer into his family. But no amount of familial devotion or sentimentality could keep Bruce from finally realizing that the printer was never going to work. And, like me, he was going to have to decide what to do with it.

Being the decent man that he is, Bruce faced the same question I had. How do you dispose of something you've given so much of your life to and from which you've received so much aggravation in return? I don't know what-all went through Bruce's mind—I rarely did—but eventually he took an interest in my earlier proposal.

My idea had been to take the printer down to the creek and blow it to pieces with a couple of shotguns. I liked the idea of demonstrating that a couple of well-armed men were still masters of the electronic world. But Bruce, like he always does, had a better idea.

There was a craftsman in town named Greg Murry who made beautiful, operational flintlock rifles. He was also a crack shot. So Bruce thought, why not let Greg and one of his beautiful hand-crafted flintlocks do the deed? I thought it was a grand idea.

On short notice, we grabbed Greg and started making plans. Greg was always ready to shoot, and he promised to have a hand-crafted, silver-engraved Tennessee rifle ready at high noon for the execution to begin. We planned to set the printer on a pedestal down by the creek behind Marty Hunt's antique store and keep the fun to ourselves.

But Marty started telling everybody about it, and all kinds of people started showing up. When Marty puts the word out, news travels fast in Leiper's Fork.

As we waited for noon to strike, Bruce prepared Old Rattler for the event by drawing bullseyes and scoring circles all over its face and sides, while Greg stood on the bank and studied the angle of approach. He wanted to make sure that the first-shot execution was thorough, immediate, and complete.

As noon approached, Bruce stood looking at his father's railroad watch. Then he nodded, and with the equanimity of a saint,

Anne Christeson

Greg proceeded to blast Old Rattler into the Sweet Hereafter. Bang! It was explosive and thrilling, and the air around Old Rattler was bathed in a cascade of multicolored ink. People were stunned, and then erupted into laughter and applause.

After Greg's electrifying first shot, people started lining up to take their turns. In quick and practiced strokes, Greg would measure a precise load of powder and shot into the rifle and demonstrate to each succeeding shooter how to handle the quick trigger. At every flat crack of the rifle and billowing cloud of smoke people would shout and cheer and laugh, intoxicated by the devastation.

Pieces of Old Rattler lay everywhere, so people could pick anything they wanted to shoot at. At least twenty-five shots were fired, and the shooting continued until the pieces of Old Rattler were too small to hit. At that point, Greg decided to stop the fun before someone started taking pot shots at Marty's sign.

At the end of it all, Old Rattler was in pieces and at rest. He wasn't rattling anymore. Afterward, Bruce stood in the colorful scattered debris and said, "It's a pity Old Rattler had to go but, damn, wasn't that fun!"

True story.

Chapter 2

Ridge Runner

For many years my friend Paul Howell helped his father Ether operate a moonshine still. Paul was a big, garrulous man when I knew him, somewhere in his sixties I'd say, who loved to sit around with me and talk about his fascinating life. He laughed often and spoke in a resonant voice that rumbled and grated like a rockslide. We had a grand time.

Shining was a traditional family activity around Leiper's Fork in those days, and many families followed the trade. They weren't flaunting the law or doing anybody any harm; they were just doing what was traditional in their culture. And they knew that moonshine was one of the few products they had that was cash-money profitable and that a lot of otherwise law-abiding citizens were willing to pay for it.

Ether and Paul were still turning out serious quantities of shine while Paul was growing up in the 1950s. According to Paul, Ether and his family would regularly cook up large vats of finished shine, pour it into jugs, and take it to Nashville in a farm truck hidden under layers of produce.

Paul Howell

In those days, everyone went up to Nashville to sell their truck produce at the farmers' market in the river bottom below the Capitol building. Most of them left home before daylight to make the long trip into the city, so Ether and his family could blend in with the others for the trip. The difference, Paul says, is that they would make a quick stop at a pre-arranged location and sell their shine to Nashville bootleggers and the operators of illegal "liquor by the drink" establishments. Compared to what they could get for their liquor, a bushel of okra didn't amount to much.

Of course, the Howells would get busted by the ATF now and then, but they often avoided capture by getting a timely tip-off from the county sheriff. As long as the sheriff was watching, there was little chance of the ATF catching the Howells red-handed. Out of frustration, the federal agents turned their attention to the sheriff and jailed him on a conspiracy charge.

Without the sheriff on watch, ATF raids on the Leiper's Fork stills began coming with little warning. The Howells could post a lookout near the still, but the lookout himself was often captured before he was able to send his warning to allow everyone else to escape. Eventually, as things got more and more chancy, the family began leaving only a few people—and finally just one—to tend the still. What had been a safe and social place where a lot of laughing and ware-sampling went on, became a lonely outpost hidden in the woods with only a single man left to guard it.

Paul usually wound up with guard duty. He was the youngest of the Howell clan—still in his teens—and he was also the fastest runner in the group. That turned out to be important.

As the raids on the stills continued, the ATF men could find and destroy Ether's still, but they were never able to catch Paul to prove who was running it. Paul knew the country like any local boy would, and he could outrun anyone in the ATF posse. He escaped time after time until he became a whispered legend around Leiper's Fork. But when the ATF heard the stories being told about how Paul could outrun and outwit them, they decided to make him regret what he was doing.

This is the way Paul tells the story.

He was snoozing at the still one summer afternoon when he heard the government agents coming, so he grabbed the valuable copper tubing out of the still and lit out into the woods.

Paul ran hard, but after a while he realized that someone was chasing him and gaining on him, stride for stride. Paul looked back and saw a young government agent dressed in a pair of silly-looking shorts and tennis shoes, running steadily and gradually overtaking him. Paul, of course, was dressed in overalls and brogans and probably hadn't worn a pair of tennis shoes in his life.

Paul says he threw the tubing into the woods, hoping the ATF man would stop to see what it was, and then he turned on the steam. But the agent did not stop and continued to close the gap between them.

Paul began taking every detour and shortcut he knew, trying to find a place to hide. He jumped fences and ran through thickets and barn yards and even tried hiding inside a milling herd of cattle. But he still could not shake the man chasing him.

Finally, with his lungs bursting, he jumped a fence, tripped over the top wire, fell into a tangle of blackberries, and couldn't get up. That, he said, was it. The young agent ran up to where Paul was lying, tangled in the briars, and Paul gasped, "Well, I guess you got me, mister. I reckon I surrender." He said the agent wasn't even breathing hard.

It turned out that the agent had been a track star in college and had been brought in specially to catch Paul. Afterward, the guy remained pretty cold-eyed about what he'd done, and he never talked to Paul before he went back to wherever he had come from. Paul says he can't remember much about him, except that he was really skinny.

A few months later, charged with all kinds of liquor-related offenses, Paul stood in front of the Honorable Frank Gray in the U.S. District Court in Nashville and told his story. He said Judge Gray listened quietly for a while, and then his lips began to twitch a little.

When Paul had finished, Judge Gray turned to the prosecuting attorney and deadpanned, "General, is that the way it happened?" The prosecutor was silent for a moment with the ATF men sitting at the table beside him. Then he said to Judge Gray, "It was something like that." He didn't seem anxious to go into further detail.

Judge Gray sank down in his chair and swiveled around toward the wall for a while. When he finally turned back around, Paul could tell he'd been laughing. But then Gray set a stern face toward Paul and gave him a stinging lecture about the rule of law and the dangers of wildcat whiskey. Paul figured he was on his way to the federal pen for a couple of years at least.

But then Gray paused and said, "In light of the extenuating circumstances of this case, I'm going to put you on probation and not send you to jail." Gray didn't specify what the extenuating circumstances were, and the prosecuting attorney didn't seem anxious to ask him.

So Paul went home, and, curiously enough, Judge Gray's sentence turned his life around, He never again worked in the whiskey business. I'm not sure he even took a drink after that.

EPILOGUE

In 1995, after Paul had told me his story, I called the ATF office in Nashville and asked if there was anyone there who might still remember Paul's case. Judge Gray had long since passed into history, but I hoped that we might find some of the old ATF agents who remembered. I'd hoped that we might arrange for them to come down to Leiper's Fork and reminisce with Paul a little. I thought we might even stage a mock foot race with the old track star. Paul thought it was a grand idea.

When I talked with the managing agent in the ATF office, he said, sure enough, he had heard the story. He said that it had become a permanent part of office lore. But unfortunately, he said, no one from that era was still working and he wouldn't be able to trace them without a lot of effort. So we laughed about it for a while and then rang off.

Paul has passed on now, but I know that what he told me is true, and I hope off in the Sweet Hereafter he is getting a chuckle out of it.

Chapter 3

Waltzing Matilda

P*ete Cummings digs into his black Gibson Les Paul and cranks out those iconic Chuck Berry chords.*

"Are you ready?" I yell, and the packed house roars. "I mean are you REALLY REALLY ready?!" And the house begins to rock.

"It's Open Mic night at Puckett's of Leiper's Fork. And we're gonna have some fun!"

By now Pete is cooking and Bob Irwin begins to rip into his guitar, and I launch into "Johnny B Goode." By now, people are dancing as the song closes:

"Someday your name is gonna be in lights
Saying 'Johnny B Goode Tonight'!"

Then I try to calm things down a little—I'm the MC for the show—welcoming everybody, explaining the house rules, and

Wayne Christeson

inviting people to grab some barbeque and beer.

Then we do one more number, another rocker, often Delbert McClinton's "Every Time I Roll the Dice." Damn, it's fun.

What follows is remarkable. People come from all over to play and sing. Many of them are from far distant places, who have come to Nashville seeking to polish their chops and possibly be discovered. Others are people from surrounding areas who just love to play.

Everybody lines up to perform, and the show is outstanding. The music is usually of very high caliber—really, really good. But I've got to be honest, some of it is pretty bad too. But the crowd supports everybody. The people recognize the courage it takes to stand up on stage and perform. The crowd responds enthusiastically because that is what the Open Mic show is all about.

Through the years, we've had performers from all over the world. On stage I usually try to encourage foreign visitors to speak to the audience in their native tongues. And it can be particularly funny when a hayseed like me tries to speak Finnish or something.

On one memorable night, a wedding party of people from

Australia came in—thirteen of them. They had been doing the honky-tonk thing on Lower Broadway in Nashville all day, and they came rocking into our place to see what our little old spot in the country was like. I greeted them when they arrived as I normally do, and I asked them about who they were and where they were from. My ears perked up as I heard their story, so I asked them if they would like to get on stage and perform something. I thought they'd be a big hit with the crowd.

"Oh, no," they said, "we couldn't do that."

But they were already feeling good when they arrived, and they had gotten to feeling even better as the show went on. So after a while, I drifted back to their table and tried again. "Come on and sing," I said. "When are you ever going to get a chance like this again? When can you tell your friends back in Brisbane that you performed on stage in Nashville?" They were all laughing by that point, and finally, one of them got up and said, "Oh, hell, let's do it!" They were beside themselves with excitement.

We cleared the stage to make room for all thirteen of them, and I lined them up across the front of the stage. But suddenly, they began to realize where they were and what they were about to do. Gradually, they all began sinking back away from the crowd until they were lined up against the back wall. From there, there was no escape.

All the while, I was introducing them to the crowd and explaining who they were. The crowd got excited, and I handed the microphone to the guy who seemed to be the Aussie in charge.

The poor guy looked absolutely poleaxed. He looked at me and out at the crowd and said, "What do we do now?" in a thick Australian accent.

I said, "Sing something!"

So the guy looked around at his friends questioningly and somebody said, "We can do that. Let's go." But then they got into a loud argument about what song they all knew. It was hilarious.

Finally I said, "Sing 'Waltzing Matilda.' Everybody knows

that!" And I turned to the crowd and yelled, "How about 'Waltzing Matilda'?" and everybody cheered.

The people on stage were still befuddled, so before they could back out, I began singing, "Once a jolly swagman camped by a billabong . . . " And they all began to sing along. They sang more and more lustily as their excitement grew, and the whole audience joined in. Everyone was looking at each other and singing and laughing. It ended with, "You'll come a-waltzing Matilda with me?" and a huge cheer.

By now, the Aussies had forgotten their stage fright and were flushed with excitement and fun. As I was escorting them off the stage, one of them stopped and said, "Stop! Wait a minute. Let's do another one!" But then they began to argue with each other again until finally they left the stage as the crowd laughed and gave them another huge cheer.

Later, as they were leaving, they stopped and told me they'd had terrific fun and now had great stories to tell their mates back at home.

Chapter 4

The Missing Link

L et me tell you about the late Ivan Walters from a nearby community even smaller than Leiper's Fork. He was called The Professor by the few people who knew him, since he was so exceptionally intelligent and odd.

Ivan carried x-rays of his skull everywhere he went, and he showed them to me once. The reason, he said, was that he believed he was linked directly to the last of the Neanderthals. He hoped one day to encounter an anthropologist who would recognize in his x-rays his rightful place as the missing link in the ascent of man. I'm not kidding.

I first met Ivan when he came into Marty Hunt's antique store one afternoon. He was there at the request of our silversmith/ gunsmith Greg Murry who had asked him to authenticate a brace of old flintlock pistols Greg was restoring. Ivan took a quick look and recognized the pistols as eighteenth century Spanish military dress pistols, never fired. He said they had been made in the Ripoll Armory in northern Spain. I was impressed that The Professor could recognize the pedigree of the pistols so quickly, but Greg told me later that Ivan could do just about anything.

You wouldn't have suspected Ivan of anything like that. He was short, soft, and paunchy, with heavy glasses and a thin Fu Manchu beard. He was soft-spoken and retiring to the point that he would take an automatic step backward when he was talking to you and would not hold your gaze for very long.

As I tend to do though, I struck up an easy conversation with him that afternoon, and somehow, we wound up talking about writing.

"I write horror," Ivan said. "Short-shorts, with a twist. I can't get them published since they are too short and too hard to understand."

I nodded my perfunctory acknowledgment. I figured Ivan wrote a little, like everyone else around here, but I didn't think any more of it than that.

Ivan sensed my lack of interest because he disappeared outside for a moment. When he came back through the door a few minutes later he was carrying a ragged manila envelope. "Here," he said, "try this." And he handed me a few sheets of typewritten prose. "Stop if you don't like it."

The story was called "Kitty-Kat," and it was remarkable. It described a young man and woman going arm in arm into a darkened house owned by the girl's crippled father. As they step through the door into the darkness, the young man begins imagining the sight of the young girl naked with her throat cut.

Whoa! I stopped right there, but Ivan had already proven that he deserved a second look, so I read on.

The girl introduces the young man to her father, who is sitting silently across the room in a rocking chair. The girl goes upstairs, leaving a scent of romance and desire in the air. The young man tries to see the father's face but cannot. All he can see is the rope-like tail of some large animal beating slowly against the floor under the chair, and he wonders what it is as he waits for the girl's return.

Upstairs, the girl leans against her bedroom door as she hears a scratchy scuffle below, and she whispers to herself, "Now! Now that you've killed him, go ahead and eat him!"

Yikes! The story was powerful, filled with atmosphere, shock, and horror, all in fewer than three pages. Almost all of it is reported through the young man's imagination or the girl's foreknowledge. Not a bit of it is graphic.

Ivan said, "Did you get it? Did you get what happened?"

I thought about it and began telling Ivan my thoughts about the psychological overtones in the story. But he looked at me like I was nuts, so I dropped the subject. I told Ivan I'd like to talk to him more about it, but he died a few years ago and I never got the chance.

Appropriately, Ivan came from a vanishingly small and almost un-locatable community out on the edge of the county. It's the sort of place that's hard to find if you're looking for it, but a place you'd surely stumble into if you were well and truly lost. Ivan lived there all his life, alone in the woods in a cabin he built himself. It seemed an apt place for a man like him to be.

I doubt that Ivan had any education beyond what a local high school could give him, but he was well-read and possessed of a vast store of knowledge.

And he thought he was the missing link in the origins of man.

And I ain't making a word of this up.

Chapter 5

Junior of Arabia

I wish I had a picture of the late Junior Walls, something that would reveal his stocky strength, the Native-American cast of his skin, and, most of all, his piercing blue eyes. He could bore a hole straight through you with those eyes if he was displeased about something. And it seems he was displeased about something most of the time.

But Junior and I always got along fine. We'd talk most mornings sitting around the table for coffee at the Country Boy, and I liked him a great deal. He was the kind of guy you'd hesitate to tell that you had a problem with a farm animal or a piece of equipment because he'd say, "Well hell, Wayne, let's just go over and take a look at it." And you'd spend the next hour or two with Junior fixing whatever problem you had.

He was an unusual and interesting guy. He was born and raised just south of Leiper's Fork in the little community of Boston. As soon as he was old enough to leave home, he started riding the professional rodeo circuit, mostly driving a team in chuckwagon races. He was good at it, and he made his living out of it for several years. He'd tell hair-raising stories about chuckwagons flipping over and crashing into fences and fights among the drivers behind the loading chutes.

He gradually got out of racing and worked cutting timber for the rest of his life. But he remained connected to the rodeo by collecting and supplying bucking stock to the promoters. He kept a small remuda at his place on Bear Creek—mostly broncos—and on rodeo weekends he would load them up on his stock trailer and drive across America to wherever the rodeo was being held, anywhere from coast to coast.

Junior developed a sharp eye for horses. He had good judgment, and he became a very successful horse trader. He was honest—as horse traders go—and he was easy to deal with. It was said that he never saw a horse he didn't like because he figured he could always sell it for more than he paid for it or, more commonly, swap something for it.

And that's how Junior Walls came to be in possession of a camel.

Nobody knew where the camel came from except that Junior had taken it in on a trade. Nobody knew why he'd want a camel in the first place, but they figured Junior must have seen a potential profit in it somehow.

Anyway, as was normal around Leiper's Fork in those days, everybody had to go down to Junior's place to stand at the fence and offer their opinions about his new camel. We watched in wonder as this weird, single-humped beast browsed through the pasture with Junior's horses. I'd never seen a camel up close before, and I don't think anyone else had either. Leaning against the fence next to me, all Ted Griggs could say was, "Ain't that a wonderment. A pure wonderment."

Well, the excitement ran down after a while, and there wasn't much talk about it. But one morning over coffee at the Country Boy, Gene Brewer asked Junior how the camel was getting along. Junior hadn't said anything about it for a while, so Gene asked him if anything was wrong.

Junior scowled and said, "That one-humped bastard is cantankerous as any animal I've ever had, spittin' on me and all. He's just plain mean."

So Gene prodded him a little further and said, "Maybe your camel don't speak English." Then he grinned and continued, "Maybe he speaks Egyptian or something."

Everybody except Junior got a big laugh out of that.

Then Junior said, "The damn thing's even been chewing the siding off my house!"

People kept aggravating Junior about it for several days, until one day Junior sat back and folded his arms over his burly chest and said, "Camel gone! Camel gone!" and he wouldn't say anything more. Sure enough, somebody drove by Junior's place that day and the camel wasn't there. Nobody knew where it had gone, and all Junior would continue saying was, "Camel gone! Camel gone!" Nothing more.

It got to be a running joke after a while—people poking at him about it and Junior repeating, "Camel gone! Camel gone!" Nothing more. Junior certainly saw the humor in it, but he never let on. "Camel gone! Camel gone," was all he'd say.

Nobody knew where the camel had gone, but the consensus around the table was that Junior had cut his losses and sent the camel to Tennessee Dressed Beef, to go to the sandy desert in the sky.

If that's what happened, it pleases me to think of some unsuspecting McDonald's patron biting into his burger without realizing he was eating part of Junior's ground-up camel.

Chapter 6

Married to
the Mob

When gunfire erupted in Umberto's Clam House, Sina
Essary watched her husband of three weeks throw over
the dinner table, absorb three bullets into his frail
body, and stumble out into Mulberry Street to die. It was April 7,
1972, in New York's Little Italy, and Sina's husband was no ordinary
victim. He was Joey Gallo—"Crazy Joe" they called him—an intellec-
tual and charismatic kingpin of the New York rackets.

Twenty years later, Sina moved to Leiper's Fork, where she took
a house next door to us and lived for several years. Over that time,
Sina and I became good friends, and I spent a lot of time talking to
her about life in New York. Eventually, she told me the story of her
marriage to the famous New York gangster Joey Gallo, and it was so
astonishing that I could not believe it. But I've now spent a lot of time
researching the story, and I find her tale to be completely credible.

Here's the way she told me the story.

Sina began her adventurous life as a pregnant nun. No kidding! She attended Catholic schools in Ohio and entered the convent of the Sisters of St. Joseph when she was only eighteen. "I was very, very religious as a youngster," she told me. So while Joey Gallo was growing up to become a mobster, Sina was preparing to take her final vows of poverty, chastity, and obedience.

But outside the convent walls on a sick leave, she got together with an old boyfriend. "Before you knew it," she said, "I was pregnant." Her short life in the convent was over.

Sina married the old boyfriend, had a child with him, divorced him, and found herself as a single mom working in an Ohio jewelry store. But her daughter, Lisa, was a theatrical prodigy. She soon became a child star on Broadway and changed Sina's life for the better.

Sina and Lisa moved to New York, where Lisa's career blossomed. Gradually, Sina fell in love with Lisa's music coach, a man who was destined to become a conductor of the New York City Opera. She wanted desperately to marry him—she still calls him "the love of my life"—but she added with a laugh, "What I didn't know was he was gay!" With a track record like that, it was perhaps inevitable that the nun would become a gangster's moll.

Joey Gallo was a Brooklyn kid, the son of a loan shark and would-be rumrunner. He became a career criminal at an early age, and though he was arrested many times as a youth, he was never sent to prison. He was convicted only once—for burglary in 1950—but when a court psychiatrist declared him paranoid-schizophrenic Joey received a suspended sentence.

Joey had flair. In 1947, he saw Richard Widmark in the film *Kiss of Death*, and with his drowsy, heavy-lidded appearance, Joey began to pattern himself after Widmark's giggling psycho Tommy Udo. He began to dress and act like Udo and could recite long passages of the movie's dialogue. But despite his theatrical posturing, Joey was still a violent and deadly man.

Joey Gallo

Writing after Joey's death, the legendary *New York Post* columnist Pete Hamill said of the young Joey: "He might have been a fresh twenty-one-year-old kid dressed in a zoot suit, but the eyes were ancient . . . eyes devoid of time or any conventional sense of pity or remorse . . . [H]e would joke with the cops and smile for the reporters, but the eyes never changed . . . tormented eyes."

In 1957, Joey became a "made" man in the Joe Profaci organization by, it was said, assassinating Albert Anastasia, one of Profaci's enemies and boss of the notorious "Murder Incorporated." According to witnesses, Anastasia was having his hair cut in a Sixth Avenue hotel when two disguised gunmen rushed through the hotel lobby, shot Anastasia dead in his chair, and escaped into the crowd. No one was ever charged with Anastasia's killing, but the story on the street was that the shooters were Crazy Joe and an accomplice named Jackie "Mad Dog" Nazarian. Tommy Udo would have been proud.

Profaci's business was run by coercion, and Joey was his top enforcer. Multiple beatings and murders were attributed to Joey during the late 1950s, and *Time* magazine claimed that he stabbed one target to death with an ice pick. But nothing against him was ever proven. The Mafia code of *omerta*—silence—protected Joey among his own.

In time, though, Joey became disenchanted with the way Profaci was dividing the family profits. So along with his two brothers and several other Profaci henchmen, he converted a Brooklyn warehouse into a fortress and launched a revolt.

As the 1950s came to a close, a gang war raged between Joey and Profaci. It was an onslaught of killings, beatings, and kidnappings. It was also successful. In the end, Joey succeeded in wresting away a significant part of Profaci's holdings.

Joey built his winnings into a small empire based on violence and extortion. For years he evaded punishment. But finally, in 1961, he was taken down for threatening to kill a Brooklyn bar owner. He was convicted of extortion and sentenced to seven-to-fourteen years in prison. The judge who sentenced him said that Joey "[has] an utter contempt for the law and is a menace to society."

Joey's time in prison was marked by the Attica riots, which he helped to settle, and at least two mob attempts on his life. But he spent most of his time profitably. He set out on a project of self-education, becoming a fine painter and reading history, art, politics, and philosophy. Then in 1971, after serving almost 10 years in jail, Joey was released and began parlaying his newfound education and refinement into a fresh image around New York. Tommy Udo was gone. In his place—as far as the outside world could see—was a well-mannered and intelligent man.

That's when he met Sina.

Even though she grew up in a large Italian-American community, Sina knew very little about the Mafia. Born into a close-knit family in Ohio, she grew up in comfortable circumstances. She attended private Catholic schools and lived a somewhat sheltered life. Her only exposure to organized crime was a story that her grandfather was beaten for standing up to a local mob for refusing to pay protection money. Sina's grandfather had a strong temperament, and

Sina inherited it.

After a short time in New York, Sina and Lisa became well known on Broadway. Lisa landed big parts in a number of plays, and the two of them became friends with some of the biggest names in show business. Soon Lisa was attending private schools, and they moved into the penthouse of an upscale apartment building at the corner of Fifth Avenue and 15th Street.

Life was good. Sina never dreamed she was about to meet—and marry—a man like Joey Gallo.

While Joey was still languishing in prison, his old enemy Joe Profaci died. Control of the Profaci mob passed to Joe Colombo, one of the "new" Mafia dons who knew something about politics and public relations. He formed an organization he called the Italian-American Civil Rights League and used it to rally support against the FBI's claim that he was a mobster.

With the League as his mouthpiece, Colombo maintained that there was no such thing as the Mafia and that he was "just an honest businessman." The League was hugely successful and so powerful that Colombo was able to win concessions from the producers of *The Godfather* about the way Italian-Americans were portrayed in the film.

The Colombo organization's racketeering remained profitable, but many of Colombo's subordinates were bridling at the way he ran the business and divided the spoils. To his hardened street enforcers, Colombo was a lightweight and a publicity seeker. Dissension in his family was building.

Into this unsettled world, Joey arrived fresh from prison, bearing a ten-year grudge against the Colombo family. Joey might have been flashing his new cleaned-up image in public, but in secret he was re-energizing the old Gallo gang. He planned to depose Colombo.

Less than six weeks after his release from prison, Joey demanded a $100,000 tribute payment from Colombo as a condition for staying away from his business. Colombo refused to pay. Instead, he placed a contract on Joey's life.

Then on June 28, 1971, only four months after Joey's release from prison, Colombo held a rally of his Italian-American Civil Rights League in Columbus Circle, just off Central Park. Thousands of people attended the noontime affair, along with the mayor and other luminaries. But as Colombo began making his way to the dais to speak, he was shot and severely wounded by a Black man later identified as one Jerome Johnson.

No one ever discovered who Johnson was working for because he was immediately shot and killed by yet another gunman who was never identified. Colombo was left in a near-vegetative state and was off the board as far as the rackets were concerned. The event made the cover of *Time* magazine the following week.

Joey maintained that the FBI was behind the Colombo attack, but most reasonable minds concluded that Joey had engineered it himself. He had a clear motive, and he was certainly capable of pulling it off. While the police and FBI looked for clues, the heirs to Colombo's power renewed the contract on Joey's life.

By July of 1971, one month before he met Sina, Joey had less than a year to live.

The obvious question is why a respectable former nun like Sina Essary would fall for a mobster with a price on his head. Sina would chuckle and say, "The story is kind of complicated."

Sina first saw Joey in her apartment building's elevator. She lived in the penthouse and Joey happened to live in an apartment downstairs. Joey was smitten with Sina, but she was not immediately attracted to him. The first few times she encountered him, with his retinue of bodyguards, she said he appeared "extremely frail and pale. He looked like an old man. He was a bag of bones." Sina didn't know that Joey still bore the marks of ten years in prison.

Still, Sina said, Joey had an attractive aspect. "You could see the remnants of what had been a strikingly handsome man in his youth," she recalled. "He had beautiful features—beautiful nose, beautiful mouth, and piercing blue eyes." And Joey had a special charisma. "People were mesmerized by him. He had that quality that attracted people to him, no matter who they were. He was extremely intelligent, and he could talk about anything. He could talk about art, theater, politics, philosophy—all the things he had been reading about in prison."

Joey launched an immediate pursuit of Sina, even though he had recently re-married his former wife, Jeffie. "Jeffie looked like a movie star," Sina remembered. But nothing stopped Joey, and during the following weeks, he began to win Sina over with gifts and plates of Italian food. Before long, their children were playing together and Sina was having dinner at Joey's apartment. Because Joey was married, Sina felt safe from a more complicated relationship.

Sina gradually learned of Joey's past, but he told her he wasn't in the rackets anymore. He still carried bodyguards out of necessity, but he was no longer strong-arming anybody. "It didn't bother me much that he had been in the Mafia," Sina said. "He told me he was through with the mob. I thought, so what, this is New York, so he's in the mob, big deal. I didn't realize who he actually was until I married him and saw my picture in the newspaper!"

What Joey really wanted, Sina said, was to get into show business. Several years earlier, Jimmy Breslin had written a comic send-up of the Mafia called *The Gang That Couldn't Shoot Straight*, supposedly based on Joey and his gangland pals. The book spawned an equally popular movie starring Jerry Orbach—that's right, the same Jerry Orbach who played Lenny Briscoe on *Law and Order*—as a Joey-like character named "Kid Sally Palumbo." Joey didn't like the way the film portrayed him, but he liked Orbach and wanted to meet him. They quickly became friends, as did Sina and Orbach's wife, Marta.

From that point forward, Joey was hooked on celebrities, and before long, they were hooked on him too. There was an aspect of danger about Joey that appealed to show business people. Being with Joey gave them a vicarious sense of living the romantic life depicted in *The Godfather*, which had just opened. The movie ushered in a public fascination with the underworld. Joey exuded excitement, and people loved it.

"He loved walking into Sardi's," Sina recalled. "You could hear a pin drop when he came in."

In addition, many people knew about the Colombo hit and the possibility that Colombo's soldiers might try to kill Joey. That gave his relationships with friends an unusual intensity. Orbach told *Time* magazine, "Joey compressed time with us because he knew. . . he might not have much time, that he could go at any minute. . . [A] minute talking to Joey was like an hour spent with someone else. . . It was startling to talk with him." Women were particularly drawn to Joey's fatal aura. "Joey was a terribly sexy person," Marta Orbach admitted to *Time*.

Pretty soon the former nun and the gangster became lovers. Sina was a beautiful twenty-nine-year-old, and soon, Joey began insisting that they get married. After a quick divorce from Jeffie, they did. The wedding was held in the Orbachs' apartment in March 1972. Joey's best man was the comedian David Steinberg, and the small ceremony was reported the next day in the pages of the *New York Post* and the *New York Daily News*.

But in three weeks Joey would be dead.

Not long after the wedding, Sina began to realize that Joey was not entirely free of his past. On April 5, 1972, three weeks after the wedding and two days before Joey died, the apartment's doorman buzzed Sina to say that a deliveryman was in the lobby with a package for her. Sina told the doorman to send the man up, but when Joey overheard her he got angry. At his instruction, two of his bodyguards intercepted the deliveryman at the elevator and attacked him, pulling a gun and choking him. "Joey feared that the package contained a bomb," Sina said, "but it turned out to be an innocent gift."

Joey blew up at Sina, throwing her into a chair and raging at her. He screamed at her never to do something like that again, with a ferocity that Joey's associates in the mob knew well. For Sina, it was an abrupt and terrifying wake-up call.

"I didn't know this was part of the deal," Sina said. "I realized there was something I didn't know about going on, there was something bigger than me. That was the day I knew it was over, that I couldn't live like that." So she threw Joey out of her apartment.

"If this is what my life with you is going to be," she told him, "you have to leave."

The following day, however—April 6, 1972—was Joey's forty-third birthday, and there was a celebration planned at the Copacabana with the Orbachs, comedian Don Rickles, and Joey's usual retinue of celebrities and hangers-on. Still intending to leave Joey, Sina nevertheless relented and agreed to go to the party with him.

Late on the evening of the sixth, Joey's group picked Lisa up from her performance in *Voices* at the Ethel Barrymore Theatre (she had third billing behind Julie Harris and Richard Kiley), and they drove to the Copa. It was a great night. Rickles introduced Lisa from the stage, and everyone sat and drank champagne until almost 4 a.m. Then the Copa closed and they all went in search of breakfast.

The party now consisted of Joey, Sina, and Lisa, along with Joey's sister and a single bodyguard, Pete "The Greek" Diapoulos. Another bodyguard, Robert "Bobby Darrow" Bongiovi, had left earlier in the evening with a woman from the Copa. By then, it was early morning, April 7, 1972.

The search for breakfast took them to Umberto's Clam House at the corner of Hester and Mulberry Streets in Little Italy. No one in the party had been to Umberto's before, but it was the only place open at that hour. "We were all sitting around a big heavy table, with Joey facing the door and Lisa and I sitting next to the wall," Sina told me.

Then without warning, several gunmen burst through the door and began firing. Accounts vary as to how many shooters were involved, but Sina swears there were five. Some of Colombo's wise guys had apparently seen Joey going into the restaurant and had rounded up some of Colombo's soldiers to put him away.

When the shooting started, Joey turned the table over to protect the others while Sina dragged Lisa to the floor and covered her with her coat. In a matter of seconds at least twenty shots were fired. Joey was struck three times—in his arm, his spine and finally in his carotid artery. He staggered out the door, followed by his assailants' fire, and collapsed on the pavement. When the shooting stopped, there were seventeen bullet holes in the wall behind Sina and Lisa's chairs, and Joey lay dying in the street.

"Joey had an intense sense of destiny," Marta Orbach said. "If he was truly marked for dying, this old fashioned way—in style—would have been a point of honor with him. Joey's death would have appealed to his sense of drama." Pete Hamill called it "a supreme New York moment."

But for Sina, huddled with her daughter on the floor of a restaurant filled with shells and screams and blood, it was anything but supreme. "I thought I was observing all this through the eyes of death," Sina said. "I thought I was dead."

Sina came to Leiper's Fork in 1991 to get away from her notoriety. She said she had become almost a novelty in New York. "I wasn't introduced to people as Sina Essary anymore," she said. "I was Joey Gallo's widow." She was besieged with requests for interviews in New York, all of which she declined. She even turned down an invitation to appear on *The Tonight Show Starring Johnny Carson*.

But she had good reasons to keep quiet. One, she said, was the possibility that she herself might be marked for murder. She had been a witness to Joey's shooting, and she might have identified the killers. For a long time afterward, she was followed by FBI agents, the NYPD, and members of the Gallo gang in what she called "an unholy alliance" to protect her from the Colombo gang. After a while, it all became too much for her and she moved to Leiper's Fork.

For Sina, the attraction of Leiper's Fork was its proximity to the entertainment business. "I felt I could practice my photography in Nashville," she said. "I had been in the business of photographing celebrities in New York, so I figured I could do it in Tennessee too."

Sina admitted, though, that her move to Leiper's Fork was also an act of "menopausal madness," which in some respects she still regretted. "I had always planned to go back to New York," she said. "I had my box at the Metropolitan Opera, my rooftop rose garden and, of course, all my friends. I kept my apartment on Fifth Avenue, thinking I might go back.

"But when I moved to Leiper's Fork, I bought a pregnant mare. When her foal was born, I fell so in love with her I knew I could never leave. I still love New York, and I cry when I think about it, but I love my horses more."

Sina did not fear the Mafia anymore. Those days had passed, and the principal actors had died. Until he died in prison, she spoke and corresponded every month with the only remaining member of the Gallo gang she knew, Bobby Bongiovi, the bodyguard who left early on the night Joey was killed. Bobby, movie-star handsome in his youth, served a life sentence in Dannemora prison for the murder of another mobster the year after Joey died. According to press accounts, when Bongiovi received his life sentence, Sina sat in the courtroom, brushing away tears.

Joey's death hastened his passing into myth. By 1976, the fallen mobster had been rehabilitated as the romantic hero of "Joey," from Bob Dylan's 1976 album *Desire*—a combination Tom Joad and Pretty Boy Floyd whose "closest friends were black men 'cause they seemed to understand / What it's like to be in society with a shackle on your hand." Soon after Sina's move to Leiper's Fork, Dylan even paid a visit to her home. They spent an afternoon discussing life in New York, shared acquaintances—and, of course, Joey.

But more measured accounts of Joey's life had revised the romantic image he carried while he was alive. He was a man capable of ruthless and remorseless brutality. His war with the Colombo family continued for a long time after he died, and several more killings took place. The ferocity of the gang war caused Jimmy Breslin to change his thoughts about the rackets, later writing that his humorous novel *The Gang That Couldn't Shoot Straight* "was the product of demented thinking."

Joey's funeral was huge, front-page news in the New York papers. Pictures showed Sina and Lisa grieving on the steps of the church. The local parish priest refused to bury Joey—probably for fear of Colombo mob reprisals.

Along the route to the cemetery, the sidewalks were jammed with people paying their respects to Joey. They strained to catch just a glimpse of his gleaming copper casket. Because of the attendance of so many gangland figures, police lined the streets and the rooftops to head off further violence.

Looking back, in the faraway seclusion of her Leiper's Fork farm—a lifetime ago from the vendettas and tangled allegiances of Little Italy—Sina said the procession would have appealed to Joey's sense of drama. Tommy Udo was dead, and Sina said, "You would have thought the Pope was passing by."

A former nun should know.

Chapter 7

God Save the Queen

R eese Smith and I were sitting in Puckett's having coffee, when a man came in who we'd never seen before. He stood out in the usual Puckett's crowd because of his appearance and the way he carried himself. He wore an expensive cattleman's hat, pressed jeans, a white shirt, a colorful waistcoat, and, most impressively, a full-length black cashmere coat. He was wearing several thousand dollars' worth of clothes, Reese estimated, and he had a look of patrician refinement about him. He was not an ordinary man.

Many strange people have passed through Leiper's Fork over the years—con men seeking their fortune in our celebrity-ridden community and people looking for stardom themselves. We've had prophets and soothsayers and one man in a long robe and sandals claiming to be Jesus. So at second look, this guy in the expensive clothes and the long cashmere coat had the appearance of one of those people.

Reese Smith

Reese and I are naturally curious men, so we decided to walk over and talk to the man. We wanted to find out who he was. I always enjoy talking to strangers in the Fork—you hear such amazing stories—and Reese, one of the nicest people in the world, can talk to anyone from the governor to a cab driver.

The guy was cordial and friendly and said he was trying to find Alison Krauss's bass player—a friend of his, he said. Reese admitted that he went to church with the man and knew him as an acquaintance. Like most of the longtime residents of the Fork, though, Reese was protective of the local celebrities who tried to live normal lives when they were at home.

So we began talking casually to the man about how he knew Ms. Krauss or her bass player. He could have been a stalker. We went on for a while, until finally the man told us he was the father of Alison Krauss's baby. He said she refused to acknowledge his paternity, and she would not allow him to see the child. He thought if he could talk to the bass player, he could locate and speak to Ms. Krauss.

He spoke clearly and candidly, and he looked so respectable that what he said seemed plausible. He certainly seemed to believe it himself.

Now I got really interested. This was a story I wanted to hear. We boxed around for a while, and then he said he had lost his wallet and had no money or gas for his truck. I told him I'd buy him a tank of gas, and Reese gave him fifty dollars just to keep him talking. But being the father of Alison Krauss's baby was all he could talk about.

Finally, Reese and I started to leave, shaking our heads. But I turned and took one last shot at the man. I asked him his name and where he was from.

He was from England, he said. But I told him he didn't sound as though he was from England. He replied that he had been brought from England to the States when he was a just a baby, and his name had been changed.

So, of course, I asked him how that had come to happen.

Then this intelligent, articulate, expensively dressed man said, with perfect candor, "I am the son of the Queen of England."

I managed to keep a straight face as he told me an incredible story about how he had been born to the Queen but he had been spirited out of England and relocated to West Texas under a different name. The Queen refused to acknowledge him despite his many efforts to contact her.

I could have stood and talked to the man all day. He was very polite and clearly living in a world of his own. But Reese was already headed for the door, and I followed.

Chapter 8

Kindygarden

The first time I laid eyes on Tom Osborn, he was chasing a pig up the middle of Bailey Road next to our house. As he passed, he stopped for a moment to introduce himself (we were new in the neighborhood) and explain that his pig had run off and that he had chased him all the way to Kingfield to get him back.

It turned out that Tom lived about a mile up the road from us, and over the years we have become good friends. He is about my age, and despite major differences in the way we were raised, we get along real well.

Tom is a character—"a caution," as the old folks would say. He has limited education, but he is highly intelligent, imaginative, and humorous. He's a big burly guy with strong blue eyes. He can work all the day long, bucking hay or shoeing horses, and then team rope with the local rodeo boys for fun. He doesn't have a regular job, since he is disabled from some sort of head injury. He is also a longtime and proud recovering alcoholic.

He's one of twelve siblings, all of whom were raised in the same little shack his parents built about 70 years ago. His parents,

Tom Osborn

Howland and Effie, are dead now and no one lives in the house anymore, but while they were there the home place was a sight to behold. It was surrounded by junked cars, trucks, buses, and discarded farm equipment. I counted 39 junked vehicles lying out in the pasture one day. Tom would say you never could tell when you might need something.

And the house was surrounded by all manner of free-range animals, including horses, a white mule, goats, chickens, and pigs (including the afore-mentioned sow).

There were remnants of fences here and there, but the animals were generally free to roam wherever they wished, which included the dirt road that ran through the property. On more than one occasion I have rounded the curve by the house and skidded to a halt because a pig was standing cross-wise in the road with no inclination to move.

And it's not unusual for one of the Osborn horses to break out and wander down the road to our barn to feast on our hay, or for his goats to escape and aggravate his wealthy neighbor.

The house was the centerpiece of it all. It was a ramshackle affair of sagging planks that appeared to have only one room. If you drove by at night you could see light shining through the holes and cracks in the walls. It had well water, but sometimes the well went dry. When that happened, Tom would take an empty tank down to the Leiper's Fork Market and fill up from their spigot.

The house had a barn, but it gradually subsided into the mud over the years. Tom's goats took to it and would perch on the remains of the tin roof like the frieze on the Parthenon.

It's important to understand that the Osborns did not live this way because they were poor or ignorant. They were by any measure fine upstanding people, and they lived there by choice. In fact, their land was so valuable that they were offered astronomical sums to sell it, but they always refused. They knew the value of a home place, particularly one where several family members were buried under a tree outside.

Tom always has a joke to tell, always funny and home-made, and he has a sly sense of ceremony. He will sometimes stop in at Marty Hunt's antique store to borrow money, just a small amount. He doesn't really need the money, but he loves presenting Marty with his pocket knife as collateral. Marty loves it too.

So, a couple of years ago, we were all sitting around the table at Puckett's when out of the blue Donneley Mealer, a world-class humorist himself, asked Tom:

"Tom, why do you reckon airplanes don't fall out of the sky?"

Tom, never short of something to say, began a rambling explanation having to do with the sun and the stars and the phases of the moon, and when he was finished, Donneley thought for a moment and then said, "Are you sure about that, Tom?"

Tom rears back and says, "Yessir, Donneley. I learnt it all in kindygarden."

Donneley's eyes widen and he says, "Why, Tom, I didn't realize you'd been to kindygarden."

Tom says, "Yessir, Donneley. My daddy always told me that a man can't get nowhere in this world without at least a kindygarden education."

"Well, did you enjoy kindygarden?"

"Sure did. They was the best seven year a my life."

"You spent seven years in kindygarden?"

"Yessir. You see, I took to learnin' pretty easy, but they was this little gal in kindygarden that I was sorta sweet on, and she was what you might call a slow learner, so I kindly hung back a couple of years to be with her. And besides, if I'd a got out on time I might of got drafted and sent to Viet Nam."

Tom's eyes gleam a little, and then he adds, "And besides that, if'n I'd gone on to first grade I'd of been in the same class with my daddy and it might of embarrassed him."

Yeah, ol' Tom's a caution.

Chapter 9

Such a Sweet Thing

A really sweet thing happened to me a few weeks ago. I was standing in Puckett's, waiting to pick up my to-go lunch, when a pair of women came in.

I didn't know them, but one was very beautiful. She appeared to be in her late seventies, with silver hair, fine features, and clear blue eyes. The other woman, much younger, appeared to be her daughter.

The lady greeted everyone as though she knew them and gave each of them a bright smile. Then she approached me and said, "I don't know you. But I'd like to!" She tapped the brim of my hat and added, "That's beautiful! You should wear it all the time."

I didn't know why she should like my ratty old Tony Joe White hat—or me, for that matter—but I was charmed, and I smiled and said, "Thank you. I do."

"You and I have a lot to talk about," she continued. "Let's talk."

We stepped away from the crowd a bit, and she began telling me fragmented stories of people I had never heard of, places she had lived, her gardens, and her favorite flowers. I could not do anything but nod my head, since what she was saying was incomprehensible to me. But she spoke with such clarity and conviction that I could not help but listen.

The stories she told made her very happy. She gazed into my eyes and smiled as she talked. She was positively radiant.

As I warmed to her and tried to respond to her stories, her daughter stepped in and whispered, "She has Alzheimer's. You don't have to talk to her."

But I was transfixed by that time and I could not imagine just walking away. I stood and gave her my full attention, nodding and murmuring agreement as she talked. Finally, though, my sack lunch arrived and it was time for me to go.

I would never be able to understand what was going on in her mind, but I knew from the certainty of her words and emotions that a vibrant, living person was still there.

I smiled and gave her a long, strong hug and said, "So good to talk to you."

She looked up into my face and said, "I love you."

Chapter 10

The Old Man

Bruce didn't cry when the Old Man died, but he sure enough tightened his jaw a little. He knew it would happen eventually, but that didn't make the pain any less.

Bruce and I were sitting in the Country Boy having lunch one late winter day, when Laura Weaver stopped and said that it looked like a horse might have died down on the Big Farm. Bruce is an old-timer, and he knew that people often mistook sleeping horses for sick or dead ones, but he also knew that Laura was a good judge of horses and was not apt to make a mistake. He was calm, but he seemed worried, like he suspected something might have happened.

The Big Farm, which is known variously as the Jimmy Small Place and the Old Sparkman Place, is a large tract of land down near Boston where Bruce kept his horses. He kept about seven mounts as I recall, a loose group he had assembled into a motley remuda over the years.

The oldest horse was named Match Point. He was thirty-three years old when Bruce acquired him, but if you looked closely you

Bruce Hunt and Curtis Stewart

could tell he had been a champion hunter/jumper in his day. He was owned by some people from Nashville who had asked Bruce to care for the horse over the final years of his life. The owners didn't expect him to last very long, and Bruce didn't either. In fact, Bruce said he didn't think the horse was strong enough to walk down to the creek for water the first time he got him out of the trailer.

But that was seven years ago. In Bruce's masterful care, and in the company of other horses, the Old Man—as Bruce had begun to call him—grew back to health and vigor. Bruce checked on him every day and cared for him as though he were an aging adult, which, like Bruce, is what he was. The Old Man required a lot more work than the other horses, but Bruce was always up to the task.

On several occasions during those years, Bruce thought he might have lost the Old Man. People would stop at his house and say that there was a dead horse lying in the pasture down at the Big Farm, but when Bruce would go and check he'd usually find that it was just the Old Man sleeping in the sun with his belly stuck out. After a while, Bruce began to think that the Old Man was aggravating him deliberately, just to draw attention to himself. He had that kind of personality.

That winter of 1996 was the coldest in fifty years. For almost two weeks in January, low temperatures ran seven below zero, and Bruce had to take food and water to the Old Man every day. In spite of the cold, the Old Man would often hide himself off in secluded parts of the farm and make Bruce tramp around in the cold and dark looking for him. Bruce laughed about it because every time he had trouble finding the Old Man he thought the horse finally must have died. But he always managed to find him and, in the end, he brought the Old Man through.

The cold spell broke in February and the sun came out and the temperature rose into the sixties for several days. It was that classic winter thaw that made us dream of spring, even though we knew there was a lot of weather still to come.

And that was when Bruce finally lost the Old Man.

When Laura told Bruce what she had seen that morning, Bruce and I drove down to the Big Farm right away. It was easy enough to laugh Laura's story off as one of the Old Man's tricks, but Bruce had a sort of intuitive concern this time and decided that we ought to take a look.

When we got to the farm, we found the worst. The Old Man was lying on his side next to the barn. He was alive, but he wasn't able to stand. It looked as though he had lain down during the night and just didn't have the strength to right himself. He had been trying, though: there was a deep gouge in the earth where he had been trying to dig enough footing to stand.

The Old Man was exhausted, but we made one more effort to get him to his feet. I got under his head and pushed while Bruce pulled on his tail, and then we both dragged his front legs around downhill to make it easier for him to stand. I'm surprised that we were able to move a 1,200-pound horse, but we did. We both knew

Bruce Hunt

that this was the Old Man's last chance.

We had made no progress after about an hour of effort, and Bruce finally concluded that he didn't have any choice but to put the Old Man down. He stood and smoked a couple of cigarettes while he thought about it, and then the two of us walked back to the truck to get his pistol.

As we walked, I thought about how hard this was going to be for Bruce. I was thinking in particular about a terrible incident the year before when one of Bruce's other horses, Buzzy, had torn his eye out on a tree limb during a storm. Bruce had been forced to shoot Buzzy, and the event was still vivid in his memory. He talked about it often. He had been talking about Buzzy that morning, in fact, while we tried to save the Old Man.

So I told Bruce that maybe we should call the vet to make a final examination and give the Old Man a painless injection if he had to go. This situation was different from what he had faced with Buzzy, I said, so maybe we ought to wait for Dr. Warren. The day was warm and sunny, and the Old Man didn't seem to be suffering very much.

Bruce didn't agree right away. He is not a man whose mind is easily changed. But when we went back to where the Old Man lay, Bruce knelt next to him and thought for a long time. And he talked again about Buzzy. I suppose I could have offered to shoot the Old Man for Bruce, but I knew I had no heart for it.

Bruce thought for a long time as he knelt, then he nodded and eased up on his arthritic knees, and we walked together back to the truck to call Dr. Warren. I don't know what changed Bruce's mind, but he seemed relieved. He looked downright compassionate at that moment, as much toward himself, I thought, as toward the Old Man.

Bruce may have felt that the Old Man after his long struggle for life deserved a quiet and dignified end, but what I really think is that Bruce could sense that he was facing a terrible and lasting pain that he might never be able to shake.

We sat in the truck while Bruce made the call, and then we just sat and talked while we waited for the doc. The sun was warm through the windshield, and the winter fields had that soft, mild look they get during the February thaw. The pastures lay like yellow and brown blankets over the sleeping earth, and we could feel life warming under the low sun. Bruce and I sat in the warmth, and we talked, and gradually the tension and pain drained away.

After a while, Dr. Warren arrived, and we walked back down to the barn. The doc looked carefully at the Old Man, and he told Bruce directly, but not bluntly, that the Old Man wasn't going to make it. He told Bruce that putting the Old Man down was the best thing Bruce could do, and he explained how the painless process worked. He was able to remove some of the responsibility from Bruce's shoulders and to reassure Bruce that the decision to put the Old Man down was the only realistic option as well as the kindest.

Bruce agreed quietly, adding that he would now be able to tell the owners that he had obtained a vet's certification that he needed to put the Old Man down. And he could tell them that the death had been induced quickly and painlessly. Those were perfectly good reasons for authorizing Dr. Warren to proceed, but I knew they didn't tell the whole story of Bruce's feelings.

Dr. Warren prepared two injections of sodium pentothal, which he said would put the Old Man into a peaceful sleep before gradually stopping his heart and breathing. As he was preparing the injections, he spoke quietly about other horses he had been called upon to put down over the past few days. The cold weather had taken so much out of the older horses, he said, that many of them were dying, as the Old Man was, of cumulative causes. He told Bruce that we could not have saved the Old Man even if we had been able to get him back on his feet: he was just too old and tired. Dr. Warren's words were straight and matter of fact, but they were not casual or cold. He knew how much this meant to Bruce.

With no delay, Dr. Warren put the two injections into a vein in the Old Man's neck. He stepped back as I continued to stroke the Old Man's nose, and after a few seconds he said that the Old Man was unconscious now. Then he and Bruce walked back to the truck while I stayed behind with the Old Man until he wasn't breathing anymore. Then I walked back to the road and joined them.

Dr. Warren made a point of standing around to talk for a while afterward, and the talking was good. Laura Weaver had also arrived by this time, and we talked of winter pasture and feeding, and Bruce told some of his funny and affectionate stories about his horses. We were like mourners standing around after a funeral, talking of nothing of any consequence, and putting our lives back in order. There was a lot of peace in the quiet air that day.

All the while, the Old Man's carcass lay over next to the barn, but it didn't seem connected with the Old Man now. The sight of the body didn't sadden or frighten us. It just seemed like a vague, innocuous bruise left from a recent emotional strain. It was a reminder, but little more.

I'm not sure what this feeling meant, but I've felt it before. When the life goes out of a body, the change is so drastic and complete that it is hard to imagine that the body was alive in the first place. And what is now missing from the body seems to have been so strong and vital that it could not possibly have depended on something as ordinary as flesh for its existence. Perhaps that is how people have imagined, simply from their everyday experience with death, the idea of an indestructible soul.

The feeling was there that day, not because the death of the Old Man had been so moving, but because it had been so ordinary and called-for. As the Old Man died, life in all its power and beauty roared around us, looking toward spring.

Chapter 11

James Holt and the Dwarf

I don't remember ever meeting James Holt. It seems as though he was always just there, on the edge of the circle at the Country Boy, smoking quietly and looking amiable. He was sallow-skinned, rheumy-eyed, and bald, and he moved very slowly. I put him in his mid- to late-sixties, but I later came to find out that he wasn't much older than I am.

He worked in a transmission shop in a spare garage behind the Farm Parts store in Franklin. Shops like that hardly exist anymore—one- or two-man operations using hand tools and working almost entirely on older American cars. The high-tech dealerships have sucked up almost everything else. So James was a throwback,

James Holt

and I wondered sometimes how he managed to make a living.

He would go to work early, after coffee and several cigarettes at the Country Boy, and he would return late to smoke and drink more coffee. He didn't say much while he sat with the rest of us, but in his dreamy, ruminative way, he seemed to enjoy listening to what other people talked about.

One reason he was quiet was that he was sick. He had emphysema from his constant smoking and rheumatism from lying on the cold concrete all day under old transmissions. He said he had high blood pressure, and he looked so jaundiced I couldn't help but wonder what else was wrong with him. People said he had been a pretty bad drinker when he was young, and there was nothing about him now that caused me to doubt it.

One day, the only people sitting at the table were James and me and Wayne Heithcock—who everybody calls "Red Dog." We were passing the time quietly when James suddenly said, "Red, I think I'm gonna write up that guitar tablature of mine and see if

I can get it published." I was surprised, but Red Dog slipped into an easy conversation with James about numbering and tunings and voicings to help advanced guitar players learn how to pick like James.

I had known James for several years by that time, but I knew nothing about this. So I listened for a while before I had a chance to ask casually, "Have you done some playing, James?" Well, yes, in fact he had, and he and Red Dog launched into tales of their early days, beginning about 1960 in a band they called the Midnight Ramblers.

Red Dog played rhythm guitar and handled the singing and, according to him, was the sex magnet for the band. James played lead in the manner of Carl Perkins, and everybody called him "Dreamboat." They played bars and roadhouses and union halls and AmVet clubs all over the South, and Red Dog said they could play just about anything anybody wanted to hear. At an appropriate moment, I asked Red Dog to refresh me on the lyrics of Don Gibson's "I'll Be A Legend in My Time," and he rolled it out flawlessly in his rich baritone.

The Midnight Ramblers went on hiatus for a time after Charlie Louvin asked James to play with the Louvin Brothers, a big-time act in those days. James took the job, with Red Dog's blessing, and he went on tour with the Louvins. He often appeared on the Opry. He didn't get along with Charlie's brother Ira, though— "the meanest man I ever met," James said, in an opinion shared by many—so James quit and came back home to Leiper's Fork and the Ramblers.

James and Red Dog played for many more years until the music passed them by and nobody wanted to hear them anymore. They were private about what they had done in their youth, but they told me many stories. I knew these men, and the easy way they told their stories convinces me that they were true.

Here is a story James told me while we were sitting alone in the Country Boy one afternoon. I relate it here as James told it, in his own idioms and accents, as best I can remember them:

"Well, they was this cat name of Bobby Keaton, steel guitar player. Lived over on Blazer Road with his daddy. Big old stocky boy, he was. They'd moved up here from Alabama so he could play. I used to go around with him ever'where, even though I was only about sixteen or seventeen at the time. We'd go up to Tootsie's and all around Lower Broad, and we'd listen to the music. We'd have a big time.

"Well, one night we's in Nashville, down on Broad, and we went into this place Bobby knew, and I mean it was packed—people ever'where, band playin' and all. But Bobby, he knowed some people settin' there at a table and he went over to see if we could set down with them. Well, they wasn't but one chair, so Bobby says to me, 'Go on up there and set at the bar. I see a spare stool right toward the end there.'

"So I went up there and sat down on the stool and started to order up a Coke. But directly I start to feel this tuggin' on my leg, and I looked down and I seen this little midget holdin' on to the side of the stool. He was so drunk he couldn't stand up and he was tryin' to pull himself up by the legs of the stool. Or maybe it was his stool and he'd fell off. I don't know.

"I got the bartender's attention and asked him for a Coke and directly that midget commenced to raisin' hell, yellin' and cussin' and all. I mean he was really drunk, and he was awful mad about somethin'. But I couldn't understand a thing he was sayin'.

"I reckon the bartender must of knowed who that midget was, 'cause when he brought me my Coke he retched acrosst the bar and slapped the cold shit out of him. Told him to shut up.

"Well, the midget didn't know what had happened, and he turned around to see who slapped him, and he seen me settin' there and hauled off and punched me straight in the gut, give it ever'thing he had, and liked to killed me—doubled me over good. He was only about this high, but he had arms this big around, and I tell you that boy was strong.

"So I retched out and threw my arms around his head and pulled him up close to me so he wouldn't be able to hit me again. But, hell, he only come up to about my waist to begin with, and he kep' on punchin' me in the gut over and over.

"I was gettin' pretty desperate by then, and I looked over at Bobby for help, but him and them other people was just settin' there lookin' at me and laughin' to beat hell. And here I was settin' with my arms around this little fart gettin' the hell beat out of me. I didn't know what to do.

"I didn't feel quite right about hittin' a midget, and besides he was a *strong* little fella. So finally I pulled back from him a little and turned a-loose of him some way, and he fell straight in the floor and couldn't get up. The bartender come around and grabbed him by the belt and dragged him over toward the door and told him to get the hell out, and he did."

James paused reflectively and then added: "You know, ever since that time I ain't cared much for midgets."

James died not long after he'd told me that story. He had a heart attack while he was sitting on his porch one fine summer afternoon.

Chapter 12

Goose and the Mailman

My friend Mike Davis became a hero last week by saving two people from a burning house. But like everything else this old Leiper's Fork boy does, it was a bit crazy.

Mike's name is Mike, of course, but most people call him by his longtime nickname, "Goose." Mike explains it this way:

"I bought me a goose one time up at the auction barn in Franklin. I must not have been more than nine or ten years old. So I had to carry it down Main Street to where my daddy's truck was parked. Well, that goose commenced to pecking at me and flogging me with his wings to the point that everybody I saw started laughing at me. After that, everybody started calling me Goose, which is all right by me."

Over the years, Goose has become something of an institution around Leiper's Fork. It's hard to say how he got his celebrity

Mike (Goose) Davis

status—longevity and personality, I guess, along with his nick-name, of course—but over the years he has become the town char-acter. Every town has one, and he's ours.

He's a big, tall man, with long blond hair and a rough yellow beard. He looks for all the world like a down-on-his-luck Alan Jackson. He's a builder by trade, and a good one. He built out a really nice tack room in our barn, and he has volunteered his ser-vices to any number of community activities over the years. He's very smart and doesn't miss much of what goes on in the Fork. I've always liked him.

Anyway, while Goose was driving into Franklin one day, he spotted a house on fire by the edge of the road. He pulled straight over into the yard and ran up and began banging on the front door. He didn't know whether there was anyone home, but there was a truck in the driveway so he kept pounding louder and louder. Finally, Goose said, a woman's face appeared at the window look-ing terrified.

You've got to understand, of course, that Goose can look pretty rough when he's been working—with his wild hair, tattered bill cap, and sleeveless work shirt. So you can imagine what this woman must have thought when she looked out and saw this wild man banging on her door. Goose said, "She probably figured I was going to rob her."

Eventually the woman opened the door and Goose began shouting, "Get out! Get out! Your house is on fire!" But the woman just stood there looking at him, terrified. Then Goose finally realized, "She don't speak no English. So I reached in the door and grabbed her by the arm and drug her outside to where she could see the fire." The woman then broke loose and ran back into the house with Goose running after her yelling, "Get out! Get out!"

The lady ran back inside, it turned out, because her husband was asleep in his underwear in the back bedroom. She and Goose roused him and they all managed to run back outside to safety. The fire had engulfed the back of the house by this time, so Goose called 9-1-1.

This is the way he describes the phone call: "That phone rang and rang and rang until finally this lady come on the line, and I said, 'There's a house on fire out here and y'all need to get out here quick!' Well, she punched some buttons or something and finally asked me where the fire was. So I told her it was on West Main right next to the school bus yard.

"Then she started asking me for the house number. She said they couldn't come out without having the house number. And I said, 'Hell, lady, it's on West Main right next to the school bus yard! Everybody knows where that is!' But the lady kept saying over and over that they had to have the house number.

"Well, hell, I didn't know what the house number was. Just right next to the school bus yard is all I knew—everybody in town knew that. But she just kept asking.

"Finally, I got fed up with her and said, 'Lady, I ain't got time to stand around here and wait for the mailman to come!' And I hung up the phone and went to see what I could do about saving the house."

It was too late, though, and everybody just stood around out in the yard and watched as the fire destroyed everything. A fire truck arrived about twenty minutes later, but the house was long gone. And the poor bereft homeowner was still standing out in the yard in his underwear.

But Goose was a genuine hero. Even Channel 5 came out to interview him about it. And he told the story just like I've said.

Chapter 13

The Leiper's Fork Chainsaw Massacre

I t was all done in the service of art. That's how I came to be standing over the rotting carcass of a deer with a chain saw in my hands.

You see, there is this woman in town named Rachael McCampbell. She is a lovely person: gracious, refined, pretty, intelligent, everything you'd want in a good friend.

And she also happens to be a fine painter. She works in many media, sometimes on large canvases, and her paintings sell well. She has worked in London, New York, Florence, and Los Angeles and has developed quite a reputation for herself.

Rachael loves animals and is concerned about the extinction of species. So she decided to do a series of paintings about threatened animals for display in a Nashville gallery. The centerpiece of the exhibit was to be a large sculpture representing all threatened species.

I am easily victimized by Rachael's charm, so I foolishly agreed to help her. I love Rachael to death, but she sure gets me into some odd scrapes from time to time.

My job, you see, was to help her find dead animal bones. *"Bones?"* you ask. But you've got to remember that this was all done in the service of art, right?

So I went to work, and right away I discovered the skull and spine of a deer in the pasture outside our house. It was picked clean, and I'd never seen it before, so I figured the dogs must have dragged it up from somewhere. I called Rachael and told her about it, and she rushed over to look at it. Just what she wanted, she said. So we manhandled the skeleton into the back of my truck and took it to her house. She was thrilled.

She still wanted more, though, and this time she wanted bones with a more bleached-out texture. That turned out to be easy enough because there were lots of white cow bones on old Preacher Thomason's land across the road from us. Preacher came by while I was picking through the bones and, of course, he asked why I wanted a bunch of old cow bones. I said, "Preacher, it's all in the service of ... well, never mind." But then I told him Rachael was involved and he understood perfectly.

Then one day, as I was driving into Franklin, I saw the decomposing body of a deer on the side of the road. I stopped to look at it and was thoroughly repulsed. The carcass looked to be several days old and had been chewed pretty drastically by scavengers. It was not pretty. But– and remember, it's all done in the service of art– I called Rachael. I figured the deer's hooves might fit into the sculpture somehow.

Rachael got real excited when I called her, so I threw the chain saw in the back of the truck and we went to look at the deer. There it lay, swollen up and half eaten, with its legs sticking out stiffly into the air. Rachael was entranced. She was so excited that she pulled her video camera out and prepared to record what we were about to do.

What we were about to do—what *I* was about to do— was cut the deer's legs off with the chain saw. I was going to do the honors while Rachael ran the camera. So I fired up the old Stihl and went to work.

The first thing that happened was that gristle and flesh began spraying from the sawblade up into my face. It stung, and boy did it stink. I didn't want to falter in front of Rachael and the camera, though, so I narrowed my eyes and kept at it.

Finally, after I had three legs off, I stood up and told Rachael that was all I was willing to do. I'd had it. I thought for a moment of offering the saw to Rachael to do the fourth leg, but that wouldn't have been nice. Besides, we were beginning to get funny looks from people passing by, and I was afraid somebody might call the cops.

We took the legs over to Rachael's house and put them on the roof of her garage to keep the dogs away. By this time they stank pretty bad, and Rachael began to think that she shouldn't use them after all. I told her that a sculpture that stank might be a pretty cool idea, original for sure. Rachael looked at me, and I looked at her, and we both burst out laughing when we realized how silly all of this was. So on the spot, Rachael made the artistic decision that stinking sculptures were not in her skill set or in her style.

But it all turned out beautifully. The sculpture, which Rachael fondly called "The Beast," was a real eye-catcher and found an immediate buyer. Our fateful bones were embedded in the base, parts of the deer spine formed the neck and skull. It was arresting, to say the least, and it was impressive. A triumph.

Some people don't believe me when I tell them this tale, but it's all true. We'd have a videotape to prove it, but Rachael was laughing so hard while she was filming that the camera shook and the video was ruined.

All in the service of art.

Chapter 14

Where the Buffalo Roam

*S*ometimes it's possible to have too many buffalo in your yard. *Just ask my next door neighbor Gene Brewer. He can tell you.*

It all started one fine spring morning when I arrived home to the sight of thirty buffalo running at a quick clip down Bailey Road. As I sat in my truck to watch, they appeared to be heading straight for our place. I figured it was a bad idea for me to drive out in front of them to try to turn them, so I sat there and watched and hoped for the best.

Then, for reasons known only to buffalo, the stampede turned, wheeled, and thundered across Mr. Brewer's cattle guard and into his front yard. Once they were out of the narrow confines of the road, they ran in every direction—up through the lawn and around his house and through Mrs. Brewer's flower gardens, and, eventually, into the far back pastures. I'm not kidding you.

Gene Brewer

Thankfully, Mrs. Brewer was not at home at the time—she would not have been amused—but I knew Gene was probably down at the Country Boy having lunch. So I returned to town and uttered a sentence that has probably never been heard in the Country Boy before or since: "Gene, you've got a herd of buffalo in your yard."

Gene reacted with aplomb—he is not a man to get panicky about anything—but we decided we'd better get on up to his place and see what might need to be done. Preacher Thomason—our across the road neighbor—was also in the Country Boy, with his farm hands Lonnie and Chris, and in the Leiper's Fork way they stepped up to help. The problem was that nobody had the slightest idea what to do.

Gene's farm covered about 100 acres, some of it timbered, some pasture, with three high hills and a couple of ponds on it. It was well enough fenced for Gene's gentle cattle, but it was unlikely to contain a herd of buffalo, who by now were probably as crazy as bees at a windowpane.

When we got to Gene's place, we were surprised to find that the buffalo had disappeared. As we gazed out over the pastures it probably crossed Gene's mind that I had been hallucinating. But we spread ourselves widely and began to search.

These semi-wild animals seemed quite capable of hiding and being quiet when they wanted to. I imagined that they were taking our measure from their hiding spot and deciding what to do. To be honest about it, I was hopeful that we would never find them.

But eventually they burst into sight. They were in a tight formation of noise and dust. For a moment, all we could do was stand and marvel as they thundered by. It was a sight of power and beauty like none of us had ever seen. They moved in unison, shoulder to shoulder, like a flock of birds. The herd had the battering power of a Roman phalanx, but it flowed gracefully down the hillside like a scrim of water over smooth rock.

Gene scratched his head and looked at us silently, pleading for help. So, of course, we all went to work. We had two pickups—Gene's and Chris's—with Preacher, me, and Lonnie on the ground. Believe me, it was a little disconcerting to be on foot near a buffalo herd. They stood as tall as we did, and they were far faster and bigger. They even made the trucks look small. And, of course, we never knew what they were thinking.

So we chased them, round and round the pastures and up and down the hills, through the timber and around the ponds. Gene and Chris tried to herd them with their trucks, but that didn't work very well. Chris would spin his truck around like a cutting horse and roar toward the herd at top speed, often in reverse, pounding the side of the door and yelling at the top of his lungs. Gene, an older man than the rest of us, drove a bit more sedately than Chris, but with the same lack of results.

Gene is somewhat hard of hearing, and he's extremely conservative politically, so all the while, he kept his truck radio blasting away at top volume on talk radio. With the bellowing of

Rush Limbaugh echoing through the pastures, lambasting the Democrats, our hopeless pursuit of the buffalo began to look like a demented demolition derby.

Those of us on the ground had the forlorn hope that we could turn an animal if he escaped the trap Gene and Chris were laying. To give ourselves more presence, we each carried a long piece of white PVC pipe that Preacher had rustled up somewhere. We would hold the pipes horizontally and wave them at the buffalo as we walked. I'd read something like it in a cowboy comic book when I was a kid, but I don't know where Preacher got it. I'm pretty sure it's not in the Bible.

Preacher also tried some of the cattle calls he used on his own cows across the road. These were high, howling cries which worked pretty well with cattle but didn't seem to interest the buffalo. I was a little worried that Preacher's cows might hear him calling and jump over their fences to join us. That was a disturbing prospect, and I was hoping Preacher had made allowances for it.

Anytime we got too close to the brutes, they would turn to face us shoulder to shoulder and snort and cough and paw the ground, and when they finally did run again, it was pure happenstance that they didn't trample one of us. I felt like one of General Pickett's men walking across the Wheat Field into the Union guns at Gettysburg.

After an afternoon of no progress, we finally gave up the chase and let them run. Gene said he was going to keep watch all night to make sure they didn't cause any more trouble, but I was so tired that I intended to get a good night's sleep and hope they stayed away from our place.

The next day, the owner of the buffalo who lived a few miles away on Bear Creek sent a crew of about six men on four-wheelers to round them up. The men roared around Gene's pastures for a while and finally chased the herd through Gene's back fence and out over the hills toward home

I'm not sure, but I think Gene later had a stern word with the owner about putting up stronger fences.

Chapter 15

The Birth of Boogie

Well, a few years ago Sam McCarthy bought himself a horse. The people who know Sam didn't know quite what to think of it, since Sam was already in his sixties and hadn't shown any interest in horses before. Oh, he'd had his kids over to our place to ride old Eustace now and then, but he had never ridden himself or seemed inclined to.

You see, Sam is a sure-fire, world-class rock and roller, and that's about all he cares about. He is an ace singer, songwriter, and guitar man, and on stage he is nothing short of spectacular. He wears his stardom lightly around Leiper's Fork, though, and everyone loves him. He's funny and smart and has a beautiful young family.

But a horse? Nobody expected that.

What happened was that Sam went down somewhere in West Tennessee and bought a walking horse mare. He called her Milly.

Boogie

Milly was pretty and sweet, but Sam was smart enough to know that he didn't know the first thing about handling her.

So he hired this cowboy named Billy Stallworth to come over and train him. Billy is from New Mexico, and Sam figured he was just what he needed. Billy and Sam spent many hours with the horse, working her on the ground and trying to teach her how to behave. After a couple of weeks, Sam got on her and began riding around the ring. Milly had a smooth easy gait, and she was beautiful. Sam was ecstatic. He'd never had his own horse to ride and now he and Milly were ready to go.

As the days passed, Sam would ride over to our place from time to time, and we'd ride around the countryside for a couple of hours. But on one of Sam's visits, my darlin' Anne looked at Milly and said, "Sam, I think that horse is pregnant!"

Well, Sam couldn't believe that, even though he'd been a little concerned that Milly was getting fat. So he had several of his friends come over to inspect Milly and offer opinions. After about

Anne Christeson

a week of that, the consensus was that Milly wasn't in foal and that my darlin' Anne was just mistaken.

But Anne insisted that Sam have a vet come look at Milly, so Sam called Danny Hargrove. Danny came over and reached up into Milly and palpated around and did all those things veterinarians do, and finally came to the conclusion that either Milly was pregnant or, as Danny put it, she had swallowed a mobile home.

Sam didn't know whether to be excited or not, though everyone else was. He realized that he was going to have to figure out what to do with a baby horse and, worse, he was going to have to stop riding Milly for a while.

Sam knew there were no studs around where he lives, so he called the man he'd bought Milly from and asked him about it. The man cleared his throat, Sam says, and then admitted, "Well, yeah, there was a stallion next door that might have gotten into her pasture for a day or two." Might have, indeed.

Well, like I said, everybody was really excited about Milly, and we were all determined to be there when the foal was born—that's always a beautiful sight. Since we didn't know when conception had occurred, nobody had a clear idea when the little colt would come.

So everybody started going over to Sam's house now and then and wagering on when it was going to happen. We'd hide out on Sam's screened porch and spy on Milly while she wandered around her lot. And we'd do things like examine her udder to see if it had "waxed up"—a pretty sure sign. We all promised each other that we'd sound the alarm if it looked like the foal was about to come.

Finally, one rainy night in December, Sam called and said Milly's water had broken and that we'd better be on our way. By the time everybody had arrived, there were several of us with flashlights out in the lot trying to see what was going on. Milly was lying on the ground groaning and thrashing around like she was about to die. She was what people call a "maiden mare," and she hadn't quite figured out what was happening.

In order to ease things along Tommy Howell and I began pulling on the foal's head and front legs to try to slide him out, while my darlin' Anne sat on Milly's head to keep her from trying to stand up. The rain was pouring down by that time, and we were freezing cold and covered with mud. There was blood and placenta everywhere, and darkness covered everything. While all this was going on, Sam was standing there looking absolutely poleaxed.

Finally, after we'd pulled and coaxed for a while, Milly delivered and the little foal popped out, slick as a seal. He was a beautiful chestnut stud colt, perfectly formed.

Over the next few days, we couldn't take our eyes off him. He would run and jump and dance like a dervish, and he was sweet as he could be.

For some reason, Sam's wife Marie wanted to call him "Boogie." Sam had wanted to name him Jethro after the Grand Ole Opry star, but Marie insisted, and Sam knew better than to argue with her. So Boogie it was.

After several months, Sam recognized that he wasn't equipped to raise the colt, so he found a nice home for him down the road. And as far as we know, Boogie is happily boogying to this day. Sam still is.

Chapter 16

Turn Your Radio On

O kay, *it's your wife's birthday, and it's time to try to figure out what to give her. You hate to go to town, and you wouldn't go to the mall on a bet. And all the places you usually shop like the hardware store and Tractor Supply and the Co-op don't carry anything your wife might like. You've got no idea how to shop at Amazon or anywhere else on your wife's computer.*

Well, turn your radio on. It's got gifts galore, and just what you want. Like this:

"I'd like to get me a old wore out beagle hound, if anybody out there's got one. You know, one's too old to run with the pack no more? And my telephone number is ***. Thank you."

"Well, now, hold on a minute there," interrupts the announcer. "What do you want an old worn-out beagle hound for?"

"Well y'see, I'm a-tryin' to raise up some new pups, an' them

young 'uns'll foller that old 'un around an' larn what they's a-sposed to larn and not go runnin' off after no wrong scents or start frolickin' around-like. Them old 'uns, they'll stick to their business and teach them young 'uns."

There you have it, almost verbatim—another entry on "Trade Time" on our local AM radio station.

"Trade Time" normally gets rolling about 9:15, depending on how many obituaries there are to read, with a short rendition of Chet Atkins's "Country Gentleman." It usually runs until about 10 or so when Brother Jerry Powers of the Pine Creek Congregation takes over for a few minutes of prayer and preaching.

Shows like "Trade Time" were once common in every little country town. I used to hear them everywhere. But in all my travels I have not heard one in years. The preachers and right- wing ranters seem to have taken over the AM airwaves, everywhere but here.

The callers on "Trade Time" are about evenly divided between blacks and whites, and the announcers know many of them by name. The informal rule is that if they succeed in selling something over the air they will bring in a homemade pie to the station. Everything I'm telling you is the absolute truth, and I can't even begin to convey the variety and richness of this show. Just the accents of the callers are enough to restore your faith in small town living.

The leading items for sale are usually vehicles, and it is a rare occasion when the vehicle was manufactured after 1995 or the asking price exceeds $3,000. Comments include: "The transmission's shot, but she's got four new tars on 'er"; or, "She's got a lotta mals on 'er, but she still runs good."

You never get the idea that the callers are exaggerating or dishonest: sometimes they'll even back track a little and add, "Well she don't actually run *real* good, but she's a real fine buy."

One man called and said, "I got a right rear fender for a 1966 Chivallay pick-up, and I thought somebody might want it. No charge."

You'll hear everything imaginable sold on "Trade Time." There'll be livestock, farm equipment, old clothes, NASCAR memorabilia, guns, pets, you name it. The listings also reflect the nature of home life around here: a mobile home furnished in "wall-to-wall shag, in lime green and brown," with furniture made out of "real wood," and an above-ground pool in the back.

A woman called wanting to sell a washer in "apricot green."

Another woman had a couch for sale and said proudly, "It ain't got no odors!"

A man called in wanting to buy an invisible fence to keep his dogs in. A little while later some wag called in and said, "I ain't got no invisible fence, but I'll be glad to sell that man some invisible fence posts—I'll even throw in some invisible post holes too!"

Animals figure prominently on the show. People will sell off entire herds of cattle, and when the weather gets cold there will be hogs for the killing. Some animals are sold in odd combinations: like a guy calling in and saying, "I got a chester drawers for sale, and a mess a goats."

Goats are always a big item, and the sellers will describe long and complicated pedigrees for them. For some reason, mules are rarely offered—maybe because they're too valuable—but horses show up from time to time.

Chickens are a big item. People say chickens are "just good to have around" for eating ticks and other vermin, and some people have big plans for starting hatcheries. But a lady called in last week and said she was looking for some laying hens and then said: "You see I was watchin' on the TV there about 'Feed the Chillun' and it showed them poor little chillun over in Africa or somewheres what don't have enough to eat, and I just thought if I could get me some hens I could get some aigs and send them to that thing on the TV."

God bless her. I wished I could have put my arm around her and taken her over to Africa and put her in charge of the whole thing—Don Quixote with an armful of hens.

Of course, in the middle of all this, there are homemade commercials. They have the 9:30 whistle blast heralding break time at the mill, and they have live interviews with Leon at the Co-op and Bill at the Farm Store and Claudine at Poyner's Tractor Repair. Best of all, they ring the bell and read the "dinner" menu for the day at Toby's Dinner Bell. It's usually something like fried chicken, chicken fried steak, fried breaded pork chops, fried okra, fried squash, fried pickles, fried fruit salad (no, I'm just kidding), and potatoes and corn muffins and a whole raft of cakes and pies for dessert. After reporting the menu the announcer pauses and exclaims, "Yum, yum!"

Some of the listings tell a sad story. You'll hear somebody selling off his whole herd of cattle or all of his farm equipment, and you can tell from his voice that he's just too old and tired to keep farming. Or you'll hear some young woman with barely suppressed anger selling a bass boat and a 280Z and a set of barbells—like the residue of a recent or imminent divorce. Perhaps the saddest are the cases of old people selling off their spouses' clothes after he or she has died. As in every case, the announcers are considerate and respectful.

Sometimes people will call and you'll hear someone shouting in the background trying to tell the person on the phone what to say. Wife, on telephone: "What was it you said . . . ?" Husband, in the background: "A 350 overhead cam." Wife: "A *what*?" (voice rising). Husband: "A 350 overhead cam, woman!" Wife: "Well then, here, *you* talk to 'im," slamming down the phone.

And, of course, the announcers are always having to tell callers to turn down their radios so as not to mess up the telephone connection. But one time, it turned out that an elderly lady's hearing aid was causing feedback, so the announcer told her to turn it off. She did, and the announcer said, "Okay, now what can we do for you?" And the lady said, "WHAT??" And the announcer said, raising his voice, "WHAT CAN WE DO FOR YOU?" "WHAT????", she says, and that's where I got to laughing so hard I couldn't listen anymore.

Turn your radio on.

Chapter 17

Leiper's Fork Vignettes

L ate in the afternoon after their work was finished, a friendly group of working men would sit with each other and have coffee at Puckett's. These were highly accomplished guys like Bruce Hunt, David Gatlin, Goose Davis, the Baker Brothers, John Gibson, Tandy Heithcock, Petie Claiborne, and a rotating cast of other people. I'd usually be there in my lawyer suit.

The guys would pass the news around and discuss the day's work, and then invariably someone would sigh and bring up a problem he was having. It could be a question of building design or a wiring question or a machine that had broken down. The subjects were liable to be anything.

There would usually be several opinions offered, and usually a good-natured dispute would arise. I'd sit and listen. To my untutored ears, these men were geniuses.

Bruce Hunt

Bruce Hunt was generally acknowledged to be the leader of the discussions and the arbiter of disputes. Bruce was smart as a whip and could do just about anything, so his judgment was widely respected around the table. Notably, he was also a fine artist.

Most days, as the conversations began to reach an impasse, Bruce would reach over and pull a napkin out of the table dispenser and begin sketching elegant diagrams about the subject under discussion. Everyone crowded around as he drew and explained what his opinion was. Then everybody else would begin to argue and scratch their heads and offer up their own ideas.

Then Bruce would reach over and begin sketching another diagram to take the other opinions into account. There was rarely an agreement reached, but everybody had a good time. Gradually, people began getting up and wandering out toward home until no one was left.

There would usually be several crumpled napkins left on the table containing Bruce's beautiful designs. How I wish I'd thought to pick them up and save them! They were the purest form of art Leiper's Fork has ever produced.

* * *

At the Leiper's Fork Yard Sale a few years ago, there was a heavy-set man who decided to buy two sets of barbells. He was pretty obese, so I figured he planned to use the barbells to turn some of that fat into muscle. He paid for his barbells, and then, holding one in each hand, headed back across the road to Mrs. Mangrum's hayfield where he had left his truck.

As he began walking toward the road, his jeans began to slip down. He kept walking, though, and they continued to slip until the crack of his ass began to show. He didn't have a free hand to pull them up, so he began walking faster and faster. In the middle of the road, the jeans slipped all the way down around his knees and he could no longer walk. He just stood there in the middle of the road, in his underwear, while he tried to figure out what to do.

By this time, people at the yard sale were standing silently and watching, wondering what the man was going to do. Finally, a deputy who was directing traffic walked out to the man and said something to him. The man reached down to set his barbells on the pavement, at which point his jeans fell down all the way to his ankles. He stood up, and the deputy said something else to him. The man reached down to his ankles and pulled his jeans back up and appeared to tighten them. In the meantime, the deputy picked up the barbells and took them over and set them down on the far side of the road. The man followed, again picked up his barbells, and headed off toward his truck.

No one at the yard sale laughed, even though it was side-splittingly funny. But I heard Tandy Heithcock say: "If that man was planning to lose some of that weight by using them barbells, I reckon they must work pretty fast. It looks like he's done lost a couple of pants sizes already."

* * *

A work crew of low-risk convicts from the county jail were cleaning up the sides of Leiper's Creek Road one day, wearing their convict-striped pants and orange safety vests. At noon, they stopped to eat lunch in the grass across the road from the Leiper's Fork Market. One of the prisoners asked the Captain if he could run across the road to the Market and get a Coke. The Captain agreed, since the man posed no risk to anyone.

So the prisoner walked over to the Market and went inside. Then he walked to the back and proceeded to take off his convict pants and vest and sneak out the back door in his boots and underwear. He took off across Pinewood Road and up into the big tract of timber that reaches for a couple of miles up toward Bending Chestnut ridge. He apparently had a lot of family living up there.

When the man didn't come back to the crew, the Captain got irritated. He walked over to the Market and asked the clerks if they had seen the man. They admitted that they had and told the Captain what had happened. They all knew the prisoner well and laughed as they described the scene.

With that, the Captain really got steamed. He stalked back across the road and got on his radio and called the sheriff. All the while, the rest of the work crew sat in the grass and laughed.

Eventually, the sheriff and his deputies came out from Franklin with his tracking dogs to try to run the prisoner down. The Captain brought the prisoner's pants out for the dogs to sniff, and everybody took off after him. The dogs picked up the scent and began leading the deputies on a merry chase through the woods.

They were making good progress, but the sheriff's dogs had also been trained as drug-sniffers. After a long run, they joyously led the deputies into a big marijuana patch hidden in the woods. The dogs were ecstatic, but the sheriff and the Captain were furious. Worse, everybody knew that the marijuana was growing on land belonging to the local county commissioner. The commissioner probably had no idea it was there, so the sheriff had to tell his men to get on with the chase and forget what they'd seen.

The prisoner eventually surrendered, but as far as I know, nobody lifted a finger against the commissioner.

Chapter 18

At the Dump

Mr. Johnson served for many years as curator for the Leiper's Fork dump. I asked him his first name once, but he became evasive, and it seemed that he preferred the respectful honorific "Mr. Johnson." He was a sweet old man, missing some teeth and a bit off-kilter, and he enforced the rules of the dump imperiously.

In those days, Mr. Johnson didn't care if you salvaged something from the dump and took it home with you. That made the dump a friendly, stop-by gathering place for people checking to see what someone else may have thrown away that they might want. On pleasant summer afternoons or cold winter mornings, people would gather there informally, lean on their pick-up beds, and talk, waiting for someone to show up with items to discard.

People would raid the bins and the junk piles, of course, but there was also a lot of direct pickup to pickup swapping that went on between people. People salvaged all kinds of things, from broken furniture to lengths of angle iron to scrap lumber. The joke was that you'd often go home with more stuff than you'd brought.

Mr. Johnson

Of course, good things never last. When the county got wind of all the fun being had, it imposed a rule with great ceremony prohibiting people from salvaging any longer. Mr. Johnson enforced the rule strictly, of course, even though he was one of the most enthusiastic salvagers of us all. The back of his truck was normally crammed with salvaged goods every day when he locked the gates at closing time and went home.

After what the county did, the salvagers began circling and descending on the loaded pickups before they reached the dump gates. You'd sometimes see a gaggle of pickups pulled off into the ditch on the side of the road leading into the dump, swapping things and carrying on as usual. Mr. Johnson sometimes stood at the gate himself to see what someone was throwing away, and if he wanted it, he'd take it out and lay it on the ground outside the gate and pick it up on his way home.

One winter morning, Bruce Hunt and I decided to clean out some of the useless junk that had accumulated around his barn.

There was a lot of stuff to dig through, and it was hard for Bruce to decide what to throw away from all his treasures. After a couple of hours of work, we finally had a full pickup load and headed for the dump. We didn't want to hang around too long and leave Bruce enough time to change his mind.

But we were hungry by then, so we stopped in at the Country Boy for lunch. Bruce parked out front and we went in and sat down. After just a few minutes, Douglas Poyner (Moon's boy) stuck his head in the door and hollered, "Hey, Bruce, do you mind if I take some of that stuff off the back of your truck?"—he knew where we were headed—and Bruce hollered back and said, "Just leave the air compressor in there, but take anything else you want."

Then we sat back and watched through the windows as Douglas cast an appraising eye into the bed of the truck and began pulling things out. In time, more people began showing up and before long, a full-scale sack of the truck was underway.

By the time Bruce and I had eaten and paid and joked with Gale for a while, there was only about half of what we had originally loaded still in the back of the truck. The rest of it had gone on to other homes, spared the final indignity of Mr. Johnson's dump.

Bruce looked into the bed and said, "Damn, I knew I should have kept that stuff!"

Chapter 19

Jail Flood

"**H**ell yes, I was there when the jail flooded! I damn near got electrocuted!"

That's the irascible Charles Ladd talking in his usual outraged voice. Charles is about seventy, a small man with a barrel chest, bone-white hair, and a face like fried bacon. He works as a farm hand in Leiper's Fork, and he's lived a hard life.

He is strong and well-muscled in his small frame, and he was renowned in his day for his willingness to fight. He frequently unleashed his wild temper against his friends and drinking buddies—he drank a lot—and, to his sorrow, he sometimes fought with officers of the law.

He still has that temper today, but it's banked now and just smoldering. When he shows it these days it's usually in the form of sharp words edged with humor. He is a man I love to talk to and always try to agree with.

Charles was involved in a murder once, though he was drunk and unconscious at the time and knew nothing about it. It happened one night when a friend of Charles was driving him home,

Charles Ladd

passed out in the back seat after a bout of drinking. But some boys from over in Grady's Hollow had a grudge against Charles's friend and had laid an ambush for him that night.

They stopped the man's car on a dark road, shot him several times through the door, and ran. They did not see Charles lying in the back seat or they might have killed him too. When the deputies arrived, they dragged Charles out of the car thinking he was dead, and it was only then that he finally woke up.

Charles's excessive drinking frequently got him into trouble with the law, and it explains why he was locked up in the Williamson County jail on the day it flooded. The jail we're talking about is the old Williamson County Jail. It's not the sleek modern "Justice Center" over in the industrial park. It's the decrepit old place on Bridge Street, down beside the Harpeth River.

As it happened, one day while Charles was being held in the drunk tank, heavy rains drove the Harpeth over its banks and sent several feet of water flooding into the jail. The building had exposed wiring, Charles says, so when the water began to rise all

The Old Jail

the inmates started climbing up onto tables and chairs to avoid electrocution. Everyone was screaming at the jailer to let them out, but the jailer said he couldn't release them until the sheriff told him to.

Charles says, "That son-of-a-bitch sheriff didn't do nothing until the TV cameras got there! Then he locked us up in shackles and pointed a shotgun at us and marched us up the street to the courthouse in front of the TV cameras. That sheriff was making out like we was murderers or something, but we wasn't nothin' but a bunch of drunks!"

It was very cold that day and Charles said everyone was soaking wet from the flood. They were sent upstairs in the courthouse to the old main courtroom and told to spend the night on the benches. They weren't given any dry clothes, not even blankets, and Charles says, "Them benches was hard!" The next morning, they were all sent back to the jail and forced to clean up the damage from the flood. Then Charles resumed serving out the balance of his sentence.

Drinking had been a problem for Charles all his life. He had received several convictions for DUI and had his license revoked more than once. Charles says the court sentenced him to treatment by a "head shrinker" one time, but it didn't do him any good. He said, "That doctor asked me how I decided when I'd had enough to drink, and I told him I quit when my money ran out. Until then, I kept on drinking."

I asked Charles how he could abide not drinking while he was in jail and why he couldn't use the jail time to try to kick his habit. Charles said, "Hell, I was still drinkin' in jail. They's people'd bring me liquor while I was out on the highway work crew." He was a gregarious and funny man and well known and popular among his friends.

While Charles was in jail, he became in danger of losing his job as a guard for a bank in Nashville. A kindly clerk at the bank who liked Charles continued to send him his paychecks, but after a while, she said she couldn't continue to do it or she'd risk her own job.

So Charles said, "I gave some shyster lawyer $100 to get me out." Charles says on the day of the hearing he walked into the courtroom and the judge said that the balance of his sentence was suspended. Nothing else was said, and Charles has no idea why he got out, but he says, "I figured some of that money went to the judge. He had an ill temper, a crippled leg, and a drinking problem hisself."

After the hearing, when the sentence had been suspended, a trusty from the jail came up to Charles and said, "Come here, I have to put the cuffs back on you."

Charles shot back, "Didn't you hear what that man said? I'm free! Keep your hands off me."

The trusty said, "Well I've got to deliver you back to the jail so your discharge can be processed and you can recover your property. You're my responsibility until then."

Charles bristled and replied, "I can take care my own self, buddy, and I can get my own self back to the jail when I'm good and ready, and I ain't ready right now!" With that, Charles says, "I walked out the door of that courtroom and nobody said another word."

His first and only stop that day was at The Shamrock, a familiar bar on Main Street just a block from the courthouse. Charles was well known and welcome in that place, and when he walked in the bartender said, "Welcome back, Charles. Anything you want is on the house," which was good, Charles said, because he didn't have a nickel. He said he sat and drank The Shamrock's free liquor for the rest of the afternoon, and when he was good and drunk he walked back over to the jail and presented himself to his captors to be discharged. He said he raised hell throughout the process and got a good laugh out of it.

Charles doesn't drink anymore these days, and mostly he stays out of trouble. But as he quietly goes about his days, you can still see events like those in his eyes.

Chapter 20

Pully Bone

It was a marriage made on a pully bone. My friend Rick Warwick told me about it, and Bernie Deal backed him up, so I guess it's true.

It seems there were two maiden sisters named Carey and Frankie Paul who lived up on Parker Branch near Leiper's Fork. Frankie was a "tall and handsome woman," according to Bernie; Carey was a little less so. This was back in the 1940s when the roads were still dirt and there was not much local industry beyond sawmilling and farming and cooking up corn, and young ladies didn't get out very much.

Frankie and Carey were the daughters of Turley Paul who, despite being blind in one eye, was one of the finest carpenters in the county. Bernie says that in his later years Turley would walk up and down the Leiper's Fork roads with his hands clasped behind his back, looking closely at every house he saw. He would pause and tilt his head back and forth like a bird to get a good one-eyed perspective, and then he would approach whoever was at home and advise him that something about his house wasn't

Rick Warwick, Williamson County Historian

constructed quite right. It made no difference to Turley Paul that the house might have been that way for decades. He had a serious sense of what was right and what wasn't in matters of carpentry.

Well, there was another, less accomplished carpenter in town named Joe Gooch. Mr. Gooch lived in a house he had built down by the creek right outside of Leiper's Fork. Turley didn't have much use for Mr. Gooch, but his daughters did—Mr. Gooch was about the only man in town who was single and had steady work.

Turley thought Mr. Gooch was lazy and imprecise in matters of carpentry, which he considered a moral failing, but as much as he resisted the idea, Turley eventually had to face the fact that Mr. Gooch provided the only promising opportunity for one of his daughters to marry and live comfortably. The problem was, he had two daughters and there was only one Mr. Gooch.

The girls would see Mr. Gooch at the market in Leiper's Fork and at church, and they would sometimes socialize with him on Sunday afternoons or after Wednesday night prayer meetings. Still, you couldn't really say there was any actual courting going on. Work was about all Mr. Gooch had a serious interest in. Besides, he was a private and modest man who wasn't one to be forward with women.

But as time passed, the subject of marriage began to come up, and eventually, Frankie and Carey and Mr. Gooch began talking about it openly. In his quiet way, Mr. Gooch didn't have much to say about his inclinations toward matrimony, except to point out the obvious fact that he couldn't marry both girls. He didn't have any other suggestions. He wouldn't even say which of the girls he preferred since he didn't want to hurt either one's feelings.

So a stalemate set in and lasted for quite some time. All the neighbors had their suggestions and speculations. Some looked to the almanac for signs and some tried to charm chance, but the signs were silent and chance didn't reveal itself either. The neighbors didn't joke or bet on the outcome as they might have if a horse race or a fist fight had been involved; this was a problem involving friends and close kinships. A serious matter.

When the solution to the impasse finally appeared, no one could say exactly where it had come from or who had suggested it. It was as though it had been there all along but had only revealed itself when the neighbors' thinking had matured enough to be able to recognize it.

The solution was a pully bone snap. Everybody had been snapping bones at Sunday dinner since they were kids, so people figured that Frankie and Carey were proficient in it and would be pretty evenly matched. That was probably true, but rumors soon spread that the girls had begun studying up on it and practicing and that Frankie had even traveled over to Flat Creek to learn from an expert.

Some thought the girls might be trying to improve their chances of winning, but others suspected just the opposite. But those were just rumors. All people really knew was that the contest was to be a single-shot, under-the-table, winner-take-all pull.

A proper bone was supplied by an unidentified chicken farmer, cooked and stripped and ready, and unexamined by either side. On the appointed day, the girls and their father, along with several attesting witnesses, gathered in Mr. Gooch's kitchen. Turley had invited the pastor from the Church of Christ to attend and lend the contest some Christian blessing, but the preacher never showed up. The preacher's absence disturbed Turley a little, since he knew as well as the preacher did that the Bible, even in its most liberal interpretation, probably frowned on gambling over matrimony.

Without any conversation or delay, the girls sat down on opposite sides of Mr. Gooch's table. Then they reached down and placed their hands underneath the table where they could not see them. Then one of the attending neighbors placed a leg of the freshly stripped bone in each one's hand, and Turley said "Go!"

There was a sharp snap from under the table, and Carey straightened up holding the long end of the bone. A brief intake of breath rustled the room as the neighbors watched Carey stare wide-eyed at the jagged end of the bone. Everyone knew that she had won.

No one seems to have recorded how Carey took the news that she had won or how Frankie felt about losing. Mr. Gooch didn't seem to care, and Turley Paul had resigned himself to whatever the outcome might be. So I guess most of them were satisfied.

I asked Rick what became of these people in their later years, before they all grew old and passed into history.

He said that Frankie, the handsome one, never got married, though as Bernie added, "It warn't for lack of tryin'." There's many a tale, they say, about Frankie's later adventures in search of a husband. But it seems she died single—if not necessarily an old maid.

Chapter 21

Bluegrass Thunderbolt

U p until the 1990s, there was a bluegrass show held down in Cave Springs, a beautiful wooded holler about ten miles south of Leiper's Fork.. The show was free and open to all comers, but most people knew that they should not try to perform unless they were known to the other players or mighty damn sure of themselves.

There was no need to advertise the occasion. People just sort of knew when it was coming up and passed the word along to their friends. Deep, serious bluegrass disciples tend to know each other as if they belong to the same church.

The people would arrive early, driving up the old holler road from Leiper's Creek. There were no seats or benches in front of the stage, so people would settle themselves under the spreading trees with their quilts and hampers and children. There was so much space under the trees that the holler never seemed crowded or noisy. We would follow Bruce Hunt's lead and drive our pick-up onto the side of a hill where we could see and hear everything.

There were never any big names who performed, as far as I know, but some of those backwoods country boys could flat play. They played bluegrass with the sort of dignity and grace that might otherwise befit a solemn or religious occasion. Even hard-driving tunes like "Little Maggie" would be done at a detached rolling tempo, releasing the wild harmonies of open tenor fifths, which give bluegrass its power. The players and listeners were reserved to the point of reverence. This music was their heritage—the Bill Monroe wellspring. There was not a "yee-haw" to be heard.

But all priceless things must come to an end, I suppose, and for a tangle of reasons the Cave Springs event was discontinued and moved up the road to Leiper's Fork. I was sad to see the old show die, but I found that in a different way the new show was just as good. Many of the old Cave Springs performers made the move to Leiper's Fork, and even the legendary Ralph Stanley appeared once. The crowd was boisterous and fun, with a modicum of drinking going on, not at all like the Cave Springs audience.

The Leiper's Fork venue was a broad pasture stretching from the front porch of Marty and Bruce Hunt's house—a rambling farmhouse dating from 1910 called "The Old Fly Place." Additional staging was built out from the porch of the house, and a sound system worked out by volunteers from Leiper's Fork like Tandy Heithcock, David Gatlin, and Goose Davis. Bruce and Marty Hunt were at the center of it, since in those days they were the heart and soul of Leiper's Fork.

The site was perfect for the show—with one exception. There weren't enough trees around the pasture to provide much shade. It was high summer, and we knew it would be hot. So we split the cost and arranged for a large tent to be erected to offer more shade. It kept the July sun off, and it also offered shelter from rain.

And sure enough, on the evening of the show we got rain. Boy

Bruce and Marty Hunt's house

did we get rain!

Right about dark, an unexpected bank of menacing clouds rolled in and rain began pouring down. The music stopped, and people came running under the tent, crowding tightly into a laughing, dripping throng. It was all part of the fun.

But the crowd quieted to a concerned murmur when the wind picked up and deafening lightning bolts began exploding around the tent. It was frightening. Then, with a flashing fireball and a tremendous roar, a lightning bolt struck the center pole of the tent. People screamed, a smell of ozone passed through the crowd, and everyone began running back into the rain to escape the tent.

Gradually, calm returned, and people could look back and see what had happened. Several people appeared to be stunned by the lightning, and one luckless young man was seen lying in the grass next to the pole trying to pull himself to his feet. People ran to him and helped him up. He was stunned and unsteady on his feet, but after he'd brushed himself off he said he was okay and stumbled out into the crowd and disappeared. No one knew who he was.

After about thirty minutes, the weather cleared and the show started up again. It turned out to be a wonderful occasion. But some of us had a nattering concern about whether there might be a liability claim made against the show by the young man who had been struck by the lightning bolt. To my mind, there would have been no merit to a claim, but that often doesn't deter some people from finding a lawyer and filing suit. Nobody had ever figured out who the young man was, so no one knew what he might do.

The promoters of the Leiper's Fork show were a casual group of community volunteers, probably unknown to the young man. But everyone knew that Bruce and Marty Hunt owned the land where the show took place and so would be a prime target for a suit.

Thankfully, several weeks went by, and nobody heard anything. Then, just about the time everyone had begun to forget about the incident, a woman appeared at Bruce and Marty's door and asked to speak to Bruce. She said she was the mother of the young man who was struck.

Uh-oh. Here it came, right there on the porch.

In his affable, kindly way, Bruce inquired after the young man's health, and the lady replied, "That's why I'm here."

Double uh-oh.

She said, "My boy has always been a troublemaker. He has always run with a bad crowd and been into drugs and crime. I always knew he would either wind up in prison or dead. But," she continued, "Ever since he got hit by that lightning bolt, his life has changed. He has stopped drugging and drinking, stopped hanging around bad influences, and brought Jesus into his life. That lightning turned his life around, and I just wanted you to know."

Somebody say Amen!

Chapter 22

A Banker's Tears: The Legacy of Burton Davis

O n Easter Sunday in 1914, Burton Davis's house burned
down. The house had been built sometime in the 1800s and,
according to one picture I've seen, was an L-shaped clap-
board farmhouse on a stone foundation, typical of rural farmsteads
of the time.

The house sat on a rise above a small creek traced by a dirt track
now known as Bailey Road. For many years it was the headquarters

for a large dairy farm. Mr. Davis worked the cows along with some tenant farmers who lived nearby, he kept the pastures open, and he undoubtedly cut a good deal of hay. Farms in those days were small industrial sites, and the work must have been backbreaking.

Following the fire that destroyed his house, Mr. Davis was determined to rebuild it. He said he had never built a house before, but he figured with the help of some neighbors he could do it.

So he and his friends set about cutting timber from the farm. Most of trees they cut, I imagine, were the tall, straight tulip poplars growing around the farm today. They hauled the raw logs five miles up to Fox's sawmill on Bending Chestnut ridge. At Fox's, the raw timber was sectioned and milled to Mr. Davis's specifications, and then it was hauled back to his house site. I assume they used mules to do the hauling, but the work was undoubtedly slow and difficult.

Mr. Davis re-built the house with a different design on the same stone foundation as his previous house. The stones in the foundation are huge, and the foundation has neither settled nor moved since it was laid well over 100 years ago.

The present house, finished in 1915, is where we now live, and have for the last thirty years. Many of the old timers still called it "The Old Burt Davis Place" when we moved in, and we have continued to call it that, even though nobody today remembers who Burt Davis was. The house itself is quite small, but it is surrounded on three sides by a deep shaded porch. The house is situated to keep it cool in the summer and, with two fireplaces, warm in the winter. There was probably no electricity in those days.

Over the years, Mr. Davis's land holdings have been broken up, but the remnants are still extensive. Two of the old tracts, ours and our neighbor's, cover about 650 acres, and they are all protected from development by conservation easements held by The Land Trust for Tennessee. It is a beautiful place, and we hope after we're gone that it will remain that way.

In about 1995, an old woman came up to the house riding in

Our house today

a friend's car. She got out with a little camera in her hand and asked, "Do you mind if I make a picture of your house?" She was petite and gray haired, quite pretty, and about ninety years old as it turned out. She said her name was Earlye Mae Conner, and that she lived in South Carolina. I told her we had no objection, but I asked her why she wanted the picture. She said, "I used to live here when I was a little girl."

I said, "Please come inside so we can talk!"

So she came in and Anne and I talked with her for over an hour as her friend waited outside in the car. It turns out that Earlye Mae had been adopted as an orphan by Mr. Davis when she was very young. She told us about the Easter morning fire, describing how the blaze had started when the long window curtains blew into the flames from the fireplace.

She told wonderful stories about life on the farm. One that I remember is that she had to pump and haul buckets of water from the well up to the house—about 100 yards away—and how she liked to wash her pet pig in the stone trough next to the well pump.

The stone watering trough is worth mentioning. It is a single piece of limestone over six feet long. I can't imagine what it took to transport it and place it there. The inside walls of the trough are perfectly symmetrical and lined by hundreds of hand-chisel marks. Perhaps Mr. Davis had a steam or gasoline drill to cut the rough trough, but the perfectly smooth interior shaping was undoubtedly done by hand. The countless tiny chisel marks are beautiful to see, and I can imagine someone sitting there hour after hour, quietly shaping the smooth and symmetrical walls, dreaming his patient dreams.

The well itself is about eight feet deep and still holds water. The cement cap on the well pump has a handprint in it, and the date 1915 scratched on it. We get our water from a much deeper well further upstream.

Then, about fifteen years after Earlye Mae's visit, sometime about 2010, a man and his wife drove up. He was a prosperous-looking man, nicely dressed and driving an expensive car. He said his name was William Jordan and that he was a banker from Dallas. He too had been adopted by Burton Davis, he said, and he wanted to visit his old home place and show his wife where he had grown up.

He was filled with stories about his life here, like sitting as a young boy on the bank beside the house and using it to climb aboard his pony. He wandered around and recognized the old well and pump and the smokehouse, though the old dairy barn had been replaced by a new horse barn. I told him the old cement floor of the milking barn was still visible, but that's all we knew about it. He couldn't remember much either.

Then, just before Mr. Jordan left, a wonderful thing happened.

A few years before Mr. Jordan's visit, we re-designed the old hired man's entrance to the house, and when the facing of the old door came off we found a large plank of gray, rough-cut wood supporting one side of the frame.

Covering the plank, in large, beautiful cursive script, were the words "Burton Davis." We decided to save it, of course, so I put a sealant on it and stowed it away in case somebody might want it someday.

Before Mr. Jordan left, I got the plank out and showed it to him and told him he could keep it. He held it in his hands for a few moments, and then this banker from Dallas began to cry.

It was the Legacy of Burton Davis.

The old Burt Davis place

Special thanks to my mentor and friend Margaret Renkl. This book would not have been possible without her encouragement of my writing.

Made in the USA
Columbia, SC
20 August 2021

43503874R00063